P9-DMY-762

An Evolving Legacy

An Evolving Legacy:

TWENTY YEARS
OF COLLECTING

at the James A. Michener Art Museum

James A. Michener Art Museum
Bucks County, Pennsylvania

Erika Jaeger-Smith
Bruce Katsiff
Constance Kimmerle
Kristy Krivitsky
Brian H. Peterson

This publication accompanies the exhibition
*An Evolving Legacy: Twenty Years of Collecting
at the James A. Michener Art Museum*
June 13, 2009–January 3, 2010

Library of Congress Control Number: 2009923051
ISBN: 9781879636224

Kristy Krivitsky: Publication Coordinator

Design: Becotte Design
Editor: Paula Brisco
Proofreader: Anita Oliva
Principal photography: Randl Bye
Printed and bound by Brilliant Graphics

Dimensions of works are cited with height preceding width.

Frontispiece: Edward W. Redfield (1869–1965)
    Fleecydale Road ca. 1930
    oil on canvas, 37½ x 49½ inches
    James A. Michener Art Museum
    Gift of the Laurent Redfield Family

CONTENTS

SPONSORS

This publication was made possible by major lead gifts from Carol and Louis Della Penna and Kathy and Ted Fernberger.

Major support was provided by Marguerite and Gerry Lenfest.

The Michener Art Museum's research and publication activities are supported by the Virginia B. and William D. Williams Endowment Fund.

Sponsors:

Thomas and Karen Buckley

Eliot and Sandra Chack

Elizabeth Leith-Ross Mow

Bonnie J. O'Boyle

Paula and Kevin Putman

In memory of Abigail Adams Silvers, M.D.

Exhibition sponsors:

Lead Sponsor: Worth & Company, Inc,

Co-Sponsor: Gratz Gallery and Conservation Studio

Additional support was provided by Steve Kalafer, Flemington Car & Truck Country Family of Dealerships; and Malmark, Inc.

Funded in part by a grant from the Pennsylvania Historical and Museum Commission

FOREWORD

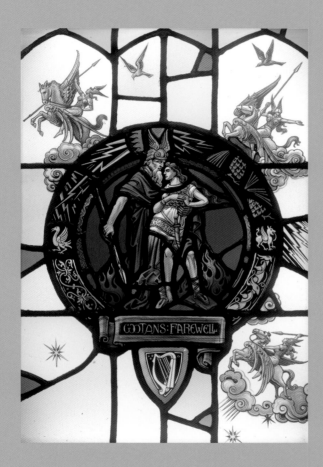

1
JOSEPH DIANO (1904–1987)
Wotan's Farewell n.d.
stained glass, 26¾ x 18 inches
James A. Michener Art Museum
Gift of Mrs. Helen Diano

On a Saturday afternoon in October of 1989, I drove my wife to the supermarket in New Hope to do the weekly shopping. Bored with the prospect of walking through grocery aisles, I stood at the entrance and read the local newspapers. I was interested to read about the departure of the founding director of the James A. Michener Arts Center, Linda Buki. I was well aware of the Michener, and had even prepared a research paper for the Bucks County Council on the Arts in the late 1970s that explored the challenges of establishing a museum in Bucks County. Later that afternoon I received a call from Herman Silverman, who asked me to come to his office the next day—Sunday—to discuss a matter of interest. Herman and I had crossed paths many times beginning in the mid-1970s when we worked together creating the Artmobile at Bucks County Community College. Mr. Silverman was one of the founding trustees of the Michener, and it was easy to guess that he was going to offer me the job of running the arts center. At the time I was chairing the Art and Music Division at Bucks County Community College, and my boss was motivating me to consider other employment.

The Michener had opened in September 1988 with a modest facility and a broad mission. Despite its humble beginnings, I believed the Michener had significant potential due to the community's rich artistic heritage, the dignity of its namesake, and the interesting site adjacent to the library and across from the Mercer Museum. After meeting with the board and reviewing the situation, I decided to take the job while initially holding on to my BCCC faculty rank and tenure. After visiting the art center to find out what the

2
CHARLES WELLS (b. 1935)
Whitman 1975
etching on paper, 25 x 19½ inches
James A. Michener Art Museum
Michener Art Endowment Challenge
Gift of Franz G. Geierhaas

future might hold for our family, my wife came home and announced: "This time you will have a real challenge!" In January 1990 I began my new job as director of the Michener. As it turned out, the personal rewards have surpassed my fondest dreams in job satisfaction as well as in service to my community.

The privilege of serving as an art museum director offers ample opportunities for rewarding work and legacy building. Many activities put a smile on my face while contributing to the goal of building a civil society. It's a joy to see yellow school buses parked out front and eager young faces passing my office doors on their way to the museum's front entrance. Working with architects to design new galleries and expand the museum's facilities offers another source of pleasure. Equally satisfying is attending an opening night, when hundreds of local folks soak in the latest exhibition or listen to an evening jazz performance. Knowing that thousands of individuals and hundreds of foundations and businesses believe in our work—and confirm that belief with financial support—is always an affirmation. It is truly a gift to be allowed to serve as the director of a regional art museum that is connected to its community and a source of pride for its citizens.

So my job at the Michener offers many rewards, but the most important and the most lasting is the work of assembling the art collection. The collection is the museum's soul. Buildings come and go, boards come and go, directors come and go, exhibitions come and go—but the collection is permanent. The art in our vault and on our walls represents a portion of this community's collective memory, its identity. And these works of art are owned not by the wealthy few but by an institution as a public trust. A collection like ours is a powerful symbol of the democratization of the arts in America. Few of us have the resources to assemble a private collection of art for our personal enjoyment, but almost everyone has access to art museums with collections that belong to the community. Museum collections make great works of art accessible to everyone, and our society is made stronger by the existence of so

many fine museums and through public ownership of our cultural heritage. *The most important task in the twenty-year history of the Michener Art Museum has been building the collection.*

So it is with great pleasure that we present this sample of more than a hundred objects that have been added to the Michener's collection during the first two decades of the museum's life. In a very real sense our success as museum professionals can be judged by the strength of the collection we've built. The selections have been governed by our mission statement, which focused our attention for the first eighteen years on art from the Bucks County region. We limited our efforts to regional artists in the hope that we would be able to assemble a collection of some worth within narrow parameters. We have always strived for balance. We have acquired work by artists from the Colonial period to the present, with no limits on media, style, or content. Recently we expanded our collecting policy to include American art in general, while still retaining our regional focus. We always seek work by artists who possess both technical skill and significant insight into the human condition. We believe that art should help us understand the world we live in, that art should arouse our senses and our passions.

Collections are built one object at a time. Many individuals have shared in the selection process, and it has been my great honor to direct the activity over the years. With the collaboration of our curators and the collections committee, we have carefully sifted through thousands of paintings, photographs, sculptures, prints, and other works of art to select the objects that now make up the Michener's permanent collection. This publication presents only a small sample, but it serves as a report card on our work. We hope that you, our visitors and fellow art lovers, will find merit in our selections and share in the pride we feel in this collection, which is our gift to our children, and to their children.

Bruce Katsiff
Director and CEO
James A. Michener Art Museum

This volume commemorates the James A. Michener Art Museum's twentieth anniversary and coincides with an exhibition that presents a selection of works highlighting the museum's first two decades of collecting. The essays and catalogue that follow tell the story of the museum's founding, the development of its collection, the people contributing to its growth, the institution's ties to the contemporary art community, and the historic ties artists of the Bucks County, Pennsylvania, region have developed and maintained with the area's remarkable landscape.

A chronicling of the Michener's collecting activity would be incomplete without a consideration of the forces that drive the collecting process. Museums build their collections through deliberative acts of selection that reflect the evolving aspirations and tastes of the community, museum staff, private collectors, and donors who have contributed to their growth. The Michener Art Museum's collecting activity focuses on art of the Bucks County region and is guided by the museum's mission to serve as a center for the study of the region's artistic traditions as well as its commitment to develop and preserve a collection as a legacy for future generations.

The Michener has amassed a permanent collection of over 2,200 objects, and this publication brings together more than 100 noteworthy works from the collection, highlighting some of its most important acquisitions and revealing many of the more interesting stories of their journey to the museum. From its earliest acquisitions of Pennsylvania impressionist paintings to the more recent addition of modern studio furniture and contemporary video art, the Michener's rich and varied collection documents the vibrant and diverse Bucks County visual arts tradition.

By partnering with artists, donors, and community organizations, the museum has focused its collecting mission on advancing knowledge and understanding of the ideas, values, and technical innovations that have shaped the region's visual arts. The body of work assembled here suggests not only the multifaceted principles, methods, ideals, and challenges underlying the formation of the Michener Art Museum's permanent collection, but also how the collecting impulse preserves our cultural history, stimulates the creation of new work, and enriches the cultural landscape.

Constance Kimmerle, Ph.D.
Curator of Collections
James A. Michener Art Museum

3
FREDERICK WILLIAM HARER (1879–1948)
Frame (known as "Spanish" frame) for Edward W. Redfield's *Fleecydale Road* ca. 1930
carved wood with gold-leaf gilding and paint
47⅛ x 58⅛ x 2½ inches
James A. Michener Art Museum
Gift of the Laurent Redfield Family

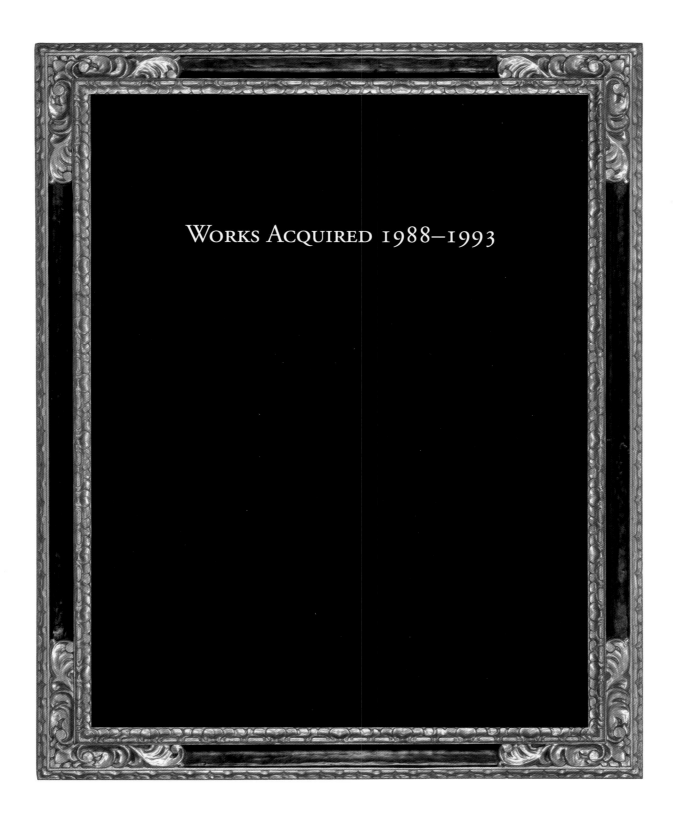

WORKS ACQUIRED 1988–1993

4
RAYMOND BARGER (1906–2001)
Transition 1965
bronze, 21 x 25 x 6 feet
James A. Michener Art Museum
Gift of the artist

TRANSITION BY RAYMOND BARGER, ACQUIRED 1989

Conversations with Bruce Katsiff

The sculpture *Transition* has become a symbol of the museum because of its prominent location in front of the Byers Gallery. One of the stories that I've been told about *Transition* revolves around Ray Barger and his efforts to secure this commission for the J. C. Penney Building in New York City, which is where the work was first installed.

At the time Barger was working for an architect in Manhattan who was commissioned to design the new headquarters for J. C. Penney. The architect proposed to Mr. Penney that a piece of sculpture be placed in front of the building. Barger wanted to be considered as the artist and promptly developed a sculptural model, which was given to the architect to present to Mr. Penney. Barger's original presentation was that of a reclining female nude. As the story goes, Mr. Penney reviewed the submission and told the architect that he could not allow such a figure to be placed in front of his building. Barger, eager to get this commission, decided that he could make some changes, so he elongated the shape and turned the female nude into an abstract form, returned it to Mr. Penney, and said, "The piece is called *Transition*." Mr. Penney liked the changes and commissioned the work for the Penney Building.

Years later Barger moved to Bucks County and took up residence in Carversville. When the J. C. Penney Building was being torn down, the Michener Museum learned of the sculpture and contacted Barger, and arrangements were made to move the piece from New York and install it here at the Michener, where it has been since 1989, the year after the museum first opened.

From a recorded conversation with
Kristy Krivitsky*, November 4, 2008*

5
RICHARD KEMBLE (1932–2007)
Another Beginning   n.d.
color woodblock print on paper, 18 x 23¾ inches
James A. Michener Art Museum
Gift of George F. Korn

6
MASAMI KODAMA (b. 1933)
Six Triangles 1966
bronze, 22½ x 53 x 21 inches; base 44 x 11 x 12 inches
James A. Michener Art Museum
Gift of Edward Rosenthal

7
HARRY GORDON (b. 1960)
Face 1982
white oak (stained), 72 x 48 x 48 inches
James A. Michener Art Museum
Gift of Philip and Muriel Berman

8
CHARLES RUDY (1904–1986)
Shorn Medusa   1959
bronze, 26 x 22 x 15 inches
James A. Michener Art Museum
Gift of Mrs. Charles Rudy

10
HOWARD BRUNNER (b. 1947)
Untitled (7924-21) 1979
gelatin silver print on paper, 12¾ x 18¾
James A. Michener Art Museum
Gift of the artist

9
WERNER DREWES (1899–1985)
Sauk 1973
woodcut on Kochi paper, 16¾ x 11⅛ inches
James A. Michener Art Museum
Michener Art Endowment Challenge
Gift of Franz Geierhaas

11
ELSIE DRIGGS (1898–1992)
Spotted Deer n.d.
watercolor and pencil on paper, 17 x 15 inches
James A. Michener Art Museum
Michener Art Endowment Challenge
Gift of Margaret B. Oschman

THE MICHENER ART ENDOWMENT CHALLENGE 1992

Conversations with Bruce Katsiff

In 1992, when the museum was finishing its first capital campaign, Jim Michener was increasingly interested in what the museum was doing. It took many years for us to convince Jim that the museum was going to be a credible place and that he would be proud to have his name attached to it. Jim's worry was that he had seen many small communities try to build a museum, and most often they were not able to sustain the effort after the founding members and their enthusiasm disappeared.

Over time he began to believe that the museum was going to survive, and he was concerned about how he might help build a collection. One evening when he was visiting from Texas and we were having a dinner party at Conti's Restaurant, which was a famous watering hole in the Doylestown community, Jim presented his idea. After dinner we were talking, and Jim said, "Bruce, I'd like to sit down with you and Herman Silverman and that lawyer, Frank Gallagher. I have an idea I want to present." One thing about Jim was that when he had something on his mind, it didn't matter where you were or when it was, what was on his mind was going to become the topic of conversation. So we left the party and listened to what Jim had to say. Jim told us that he had watched with interest the development of the museum and he wanted to help the museum build the collection. In order to do that, he planned to create a challenge grant, but his grant was going to be unique: he would challenge the *community* to give pictures to match a cash gift that he would give to support the museum's endowment. He basically spelled the idea out that evening, and then over the course of the next several months we worked out the details.

The plan was ultimately called the Michener Art Endowment Challenge. Jim would make a $500,000 contribution to the museum's endowment if citizens from the community would donate forty museum-quality artworks to our collection. Jim was smart and didn't trust the museum to say that we had received forty museum-quality pictures, so we had to set up an independent arbiter who would decide whether or not we had reached our goal. The individual selected for that function was Pete Biester, a member of the museum's board and a county judge whom Jim respected. When people made gifts to the museum, Pete decided whether they were museum quality and if they counted toward the forty pictures that we had to acquire.

We developed a specific list of artists whose work would meet the criteria of the endowment challenge, and Jim helped us promote this program. In the early 1990s Jim Michener was still a national figure, and you could get press attention for things that he did. Eventually an Associated Press wire story about the challenge grant was printed, and we received press from all around the country. When all was said and done, the museum took in 189 works of art for the collection and still had $500,000 in the endowment to help cover operating costs. Jim's challenge was a success beyond any of our dreams.

From a recorded conversation with
Kristy Krivitsky, *October 29, 2008*

12
CLARENCE HOLBROOK CARTER (1904–2000)
Over and Above Series (Fox) 1963
pencil, gouache, and feathers on paper, 29½ x 21½ inches
James A. Michener Art Museum
Michener Art Endowment Challenge
Gift of Mr. Wm. A. and Anne Stetson Rawak

13
JANE TELLER (1911–1990)
Celebration Totem 1978
maple, beech, oak, hemlock wood, 91 x 40 x 38½ inches
James A. Michener Art Museum
Gift of Ms. Eleanor Denoon

14
PAUL KEENE (b. 1920)
Variation on a Flute Player (Icon Series) 1985
acrylic on paper, 41¼ x 29½ inches
James A. Michener Art Museum
Museum purchase

15
LAWRENCE CALCAGNO (1913–1993)
June 1961 1961
oil on canvas, 59½ x 47½ inches
James A. Michener Art Museum
Gift of Mari and James A. Michener

16
HENRY B. SNELL (1858–1943)
The Barber's Shop n.d.
oil on canvas, 25 x 30 inches
James A. Michener Art Museum
Michener Art Endowment Challenge
Gift of D. Kenneth Leiby

The Barber's Shop by Henry B. Snell, Acquired 1992

Conversations with Bruce Katsiff

When the museum was attempting to secure donations for the Michener Art Endowment Challenge, one of the people I started to visit was a remarkable elderly gentleman by the name of Dr. Kenneth Leiby. Dr. Leiby moved to New Hope in the 1930s to become a general practitioner in the community. He lived in a large Victorian house right on Main Street near Bridge Street—his house has now become the Mansion Inn. Dr. Leiby used to proudly talk about the fact that he had delivered over five thousand babies in the river valley during his career. Many well-known artists from the community were his patients, and he would often trade medical services for pictures. Dr. Leiby had built a collection of Pennsylvania impressionist works over the course of his career, and needless to say we were interested in seeing if Dr. Leiby might donate these works to the museum.

Dr. Leiby was very fond of Jim Michener. He had never met Jim, but he had been a fan and had read much of his work. I was able to bring Dr. Leiby autographed books and other objects, which he enjoyed, and we began to talk about the possibility of donating his collection to the museum. Eventually Dr. Leiby made the decision to give the museum fourteen works.

The story of Henry Snell's *The Barber's Shop* is one of the most poignant stories of the doctor's acquisitions. Dr. Leiby told me he was with Mr. and Mrs. Snell in their apartment, which was on the upper floor of a building at the corner of Bridge and Main streets in New Hope,

when Henry Snell died. Above the couch in the living room hung a painting by Snell of the view seen from Snell's window, which included a view of Dr. Leiby's house. Mrs. Snell, moved by the events of the afternoon, went up to the picture, simply took it off the wall, handed it to Dr. Leiby, and said: "Dr. Leiby, Henry would want thee to have this." This story is indicative of relationships forged between artists of our community and the folks who live here.

I have come to understand that Dr. Leiby's gift to the museum made him a happy man. He was thrilled with the idea that he could give his collection to a public institution and that it would be enjoyed for years to come by thousands of individuals. Dr. Leiby's act of public generosity has been repeated by hundreds of like-minded citizens.

From a recorded conversation with
Kristy Krivitsky, *October 29, 2008*

19
Unknown
View of Almshouse ca. 1900
oil on canvas, 24 x 30⅛ inches
James A. Michener Art Museum
Anonymous Gift

20
WILLIAM LANGSON LATHROP (1859–1938)
Untitled (Landscape with Figure) ca. 1897
oil on canvas, 19 x 25 inches
James A. Michener Art Museum
Michener Art Endowment Challenge
Gift of Malcolm and Eleanor Polis

21
KATHARINE STEELE RENNINGER (1925–2004)
Morrell's Spinning Wheel and Wool Winder   1988
casein on linen canvas mounted on Masonite, 17⅝ x 23⅝ inches
James A. Michener Art Museum
Gift of Mr. and Mrs. Joseph L. Wesley Sr.,
on the occasion of a tribute to George Ermentrout

22
CHARLES CHILD (1902–1983)
Study for the Bucks County Playhouse Stage Curtain   ca. 1939
ink and watercolor on paper, 24½ x 36½ inches
James A. Michener Art Museum
Michener Art Endowment Challenge
Gift of Barbara S. and Sol Jacobson

23

George Nakashima Memorial Reading Room
installed in 1993 in honor of George Nakashima
furnishings by Mira Nakashima-Yarnall (b. 1942):
Coffee Table, claro walnut burl, 1993
Conoid Lounge Chairs, claro and English walnut, 1993
Open Back Bookshelf, cherry, 1993
Asa-no-ha Wall Cabinet, walnut, 1993
Hanging Wall Shelf, walnut, 1993
Shoji Screens, white cedar and fiberglass, 1993

William A. Smith (1918–1989)
Portrait of George Nakashima 1988–89
oil on canvas, 43¾ x 41¼
James A. Michener Art Museum
Gift of Kevin Nakashima and Mira Nakashima-Yarnall

Mary Brombacher Bowman *Bamboo Scroll* 1998 (not pictured)
watercolor on rice paper, mounted on silk and cloth, 43 x 17 inches
James A. Michener Art Museum. Gift of the artist

GEORGE NAKASHIMA MEMORIAL READING ROOM 1993

Conversations with Bruce Katsiff

When we were planning our initial expansion in 1990, one of my activities was to go around and visit museums in the region that had recently completed expansion projects. I wanted to get a feel for what was being done and come up with new ideas for the Michener. One feature I saw at the Princeton University Museum was a reading room, which was a space off the galleries where people could go and read a catalogue or rest. I thought this was an interesting idea, and it stimulated the notion of doing something similar here.

To me the obvious choice was to plan a room around the work of George Nakashima. I had a discussion with the architect, Lynn Taylor, and he suggested we approach George Nakashima's daughter, Mira, and propose that she undertake the design of a room. Lynn determined the shape of the room and its location, but we wanted the family to design the entire environment—both the actual furniture and the space itself. They were delighted with the idea.

Mira came up with a splendid design that incorporated some basic elements of a traditional Japanese space, including the use of a mother post to hold up the corner of the room. We ended up selecting a tree from the Nakashima property, which the engineers needed to approve because a piece of steel had been originally planned. At one point we considered using traditional tatami mats, which would mean visitors would have to take their shoes off before they entered the room. Finally our interior designer suggested sisal carpet, which would offer the feel of a tatami mat without posing the difficulty of making folks remove their shoes.

The cabinet in the room has always amused me. It was one of our mistakes, which we overcame after the room was finished. When we originally planned the space, we asked Mira to design a unique cabinet that would hold a television to show videos on our current exhibitions. After we built the room and took a look at it, we decided that it was a spiritual space and that any media would destroy its quiet and solitude. So Mira's cabinet is still there, but the television has never been used.

Many people I encounter talk about their wonderful experiences in the space. We were very pleased that the Nakashimas committed to undertake the project. The Nakashima Room is clearly one of the jewels of the Michener Museum.

From a recorded conversation with
Kristy Krivitsky, *November 4, 2008*

24
SELMA BORTNER (b. 1926)
Aida and the Mirror   1990
linoleum print on paper, 30 x 36 inches
James A. Michener Art Museum
Museum purchase funded by an Anonymous Donor
from the Bucks Biennial I Exhibition

Building a Collection

Constance Kimmerle

In its first two decades, the James A. Michener Art Museum has amassed a permanent collection of over 2,200 objects that sample the Bucks County region's rich artistic and cultural heritage. From Jonathan Trego's mid-nineteenth-century portraits that reveal the impact of Quaker values on the Bucks County portrait tradition, to Edward W. Redfield's robust scenes of nature that are a welcome counterbalance to the ephemeral, virtual experiences that surround us today, to the family photographs of Emmet Gowin that explore the connection between our feelings and the minute details of our physical experience, the Michener Art Museum's permanent collection documents the changing relationships of artists to their physical and cultural environments as well as the technical and conceptual innovations that are part of the colorful history of Bucks County's visual arts.

INSTITUTIONAL GOALS AND EARLY COLLECTIONS PLANNING: A VISION EMERGES

The Michener Art Museum opened in 1988, at a time when Americans were reassessing the role of museums and their collections. During the 1990s, the first decade of the Michener's existence, American museum attendance grew by over two hundred million visitors so that museums became the most popular cultural institutions in America.[1] As new audiences came through the doors, museum staffs and trustees began discussions about the kind of experiences visitors were seeking and whether physical objects could compete with digital technologies and the virtual world's impact on the ways individuals access information and entertainment. Was the essence of a museum found in its collections, or in its role as a learning/experience environment? As questions and challenges mounted against the traditional role of the museum as a repository of rare and beautiful objects, museums began reassessing the value judgments and criteria behind their collecting policies.

James Michener, the Michener Art Museum's namesake, had definite ideas about museum collections and the role of the private collector in building museum collections. Recognizing that evolving tastes and dynamic pressures underpin a museum's selections when building a collection, Michener singled out the private collector's civic responsibility as essential to preservation of art in a modern democratic society.

> I had not been collecting American paintings for long before I perceived that the role of the private collector in a democracy is a very particular one and quite essential to the preservation of art. To be specific, I think the private collector is needed because he can acquire works of art without regard to public opinion . . . the private collector is responsible for combing the field of his contemporaries and finding out for himself what is good and acquiring it for the use of future generations.
>
> . . . He is protecting the curator against the passage of time when all the good examples of an artist's work have disappeared and are no longer available to museums. The private collector ought to be prowling the frontier and doing those things which he alone can do well . . . gambling his interests against the future and making contacts with immortality, which the public curator is not always free to do. . . .[2]

It may have been Michener's Quaker background that made him aware of civic responsibility in preserving a community's artistic heritage. This emphasis on civic duty was critical to the success of his 1992 Michener Art Endowment Challenge strategy, which was designed to support the early collecting efforts of the Michener Art Museum. Mindful of the powerful role museum collections exert as conveyors of ideas and values, Michener understood that collections are cultural expressions in their own right, "showing the flaws as well as the accomplishments" and "the grandeur and nonsense" of their respective period of formation:

> I have rummaged in too many museum storerooms to believe that reputations in art are permanent, that tastes do not change radically and rapidly. . . . I suspect, from this experience, that one of these days there will be a sharp reevaluation on American painting in this century. Artists whose reputations I respected and whose work I liked and acquired will be judged by the critics to have been rather small beer, while others whom I overlooked will be found to have been closer to the central tendency of the age than I supposed.
>
> The significant point is that I have found throughout the world that whenever a museum collected the best work done in any period, that collection always retained considerable intellectual interest, regardless of where in the hierarchy of values the period itself came to rest.[3]

The idea for a regional museum devoted to collecting and preserving the works of Bucks County's artistic traditions and values can be traced to the 1960s, when such public-spirited citizens as James Michener began efforts to establish a museum. His idea took root in 1974 with the founding of the Bucks County Council on the Arts, a nonprofit volunteer group devoted to promoting the arts in Bucks County. With support of the County Commissioners, Herman Silverman, and the board of the BCCA, funding was appropriated to convert the abandoned Bucks County jail into a facility to house the James A. Michener Arts Center. Designed by Addison Hutton in 1884, the former Bucks County prison complex had been modeled after John Haviland's Quaker-inspired radial design for prison architecture, in which prisoners were kept in solitude and rehabilitation was linked to the belief that solitary confinement enhanced prisoners' penitence for their criminal behavior.

With a substantial endowment gift provided by Michener himself, the Michener Arts Center opened in September 1988. The new art center defined its mission as exhibiting and promoting the arts for the benefit of the public through its collection of twentieth-century American art, its temporary exhibitions, and its cultural programs.[4] With Linda Buki as director, the center established its collecting criteria as limited either to work created by American artists with national recognition or to the work of significant Bucks County artists who had received recognition outside the Delaware Valley region. Landscape was a predominant theme in the inaugural exhibition, which featured fifteen paintings from Mari and James Michener's mid-century American art collection as well as twenty Pennsylvania impressionist landscapes and eight outdoor sculptures by regional artists. The art center's first acquisitions included mainly landscapes, primarily of Bucks County scenes. Among these works was a landscape of the Bucks County Almshouse by an unknown artist (*View of Almshouse*, ca. 1900; pl. 19), rendered in a topographical style typical of America's earliest landscape paintings that depict specific features of a site or terrain for local residents. Other acquisitions from the Michener's opening year included regional landscapes by the Pennsylvania impressionists John Folinsbee, Walter Baum, and Fern Coppedge.

The following year, 1989, the Michener hosted a retrospective of the work of master woodworker and furniture maker George Nakashima and added to its permanent collection a significant study collection of Charles Rudy sculpture, composed of plasters, plaster molds, associated rubber molds, and plaster positives, as well as tools that document the working methods of the nationally recognized sculptor.[5] The museum received two sculptures that would be exhibited on its grounds for the next two decades: Raymond Barger's monumental bronze *Transition*, originally commissioned for the J. C. Penney headquarters building in New York City (1965; pl. 4), and Harry Gordon's oak sculpture *Face* (1982; pl. 7).

In 1990 Bruce Katsiff, former chair of the Art and Music Division at Bucks County Community College, assumed the director's position. As an educator and artist, he envisioned the museum's role in terms of its capacity to deliver educational and aesthetic experiences that influence the way people view the potential of their lives and that of their community, and he encouraged the museum through its collections, exhibitions, programmatic events, and outreach projects to offer visitors opportunities for dialogue and reflection on the relation of regional art to the community. That year, 1990, the museum hosted twelve exhibitions, including a retrospective of Fern Coppedge and a survey of the Pennsylvania impressionists; and the permanent collection expanded to include works by Coppedge (*The Road to Lumberville*, 1938; pl. 18), Faye Badura, John Foster, Paul Sisko, and Alan Magee.

Within two years of its opening, the Michener Arts Center changed its name to the James A. Michener Art Museum, and in 1991 the museum revised its mission statement to define the institution as a focal point for the visual arts in Bucks County with the purpose of collecting, preserving, interpreting, and exhibiting art of the Bucks County region and American sculpture.[6] Acquisitions for 1991 included sculptures by Jane Teller (*Celebration Totem*, 1978; pl. 13) and Greg Wyatt, paintings by Paul Keene (*Variation on a Flute Player*, 1985; pl. 14) and Louis Stone, and stained glass by Joseph Diano (*Wotan's Farewell*, n.d.; pl. 1). The Michener hosted a retrospective of the work of contemporary artist Alan Magee as well as an exhibition about the twentieth-century modernist movement that had emerged in the New Hope region as early as the teens.

In 1992 the museum organized its first Bucks County Artists Biennial, a juried exhibition of the work of some thirty regional contemporary artists. At the suggestion of James Michener, the museum purchased three works from the show: Selma Bortner's *Aida and the Mirror* (1990; pl. 24), Marlene Miller's charcoal drawing *Broadway Baby Says Goodnight*, and Robert Dodge's painting *Far into Friday*. The museum also acquired six woodblock prints by Richard Kemble (*Another Beginning*, n.d.; pl. 5).

The Michener embarked on a major collections-building program in 1992, prompted by James Michener's challenge and pledge of

$500,000 to the museum's endowment. Michener's gift was conditioned on the institution's ability to attract from individual donors forty museum-quality works appropriate to its collecting interests. The collections committee, headed by Edward G. Biester Jr., ultimately prepared a list of twenty-four artists as a tool to leverage donations. More than half the artists on the list were those affiliated with the Pennsylvania impressionist landscape group. The list also included nineteenth-century artists Edward Hicks, Thomas Hicks, Martin Johnson Heade, Thomas Otter, Jonathan K. Trego, and William B. T. Trego as well as twentieth-century modernist artists such as R.A.D. Miller, Elsie Driggs, Lee Gatch, Lloyd Ney, B.J.O. Nordfeldt, Charles Sheeler, Morton Schamberg, and George Nakashima. The challenge grant resulted in the acquisition of 189 works (forty-six paintings, eight sculptures, two decorative art objects, one book, and 132 works on paper) from fifty-five donors, including works by Edward W. Redfield, Daniel Garber, M. Elizabeth Price, Paul Keene, and George Nakashima. More than half the paintings donated were landscapes, with a majority of the paper-based works being drawings and etchings by Daniel Garber (five drawings and fifty-three etchings, as well as a comprehensive set of platinum photographs of his work, including photographs of destroyed canvases). Bucks County family practitioner Dr. D. Kenneth Leiby donated fourteen works, many of which he had received in exchange for his medical services to artists like Daniel Garber, M. Elizabeth Price, Harry Leith-Ross, and George Sotter. Amassing a significant collection of Pennsylvania impressionist works over his career, Leiby noted that he had never presented Daniel Garber with a bill during all the years that he treated him, adding that he had been amply rewarded with art.

AN INTELLECTUAL FRAMEWORK FOR COLLECTIONS

While the Michener Art Museum's collecting focus is determined by its mission, the nature and content of its collections have been shaped by compelling ideas, values, technical innovations,

and economic forces that have defined the region's artistic and cultural heritage. The region's visual arts were influenced early on by the ideals and values of its Quaker inhabitants who not only embraced the rural landscape as a subject worthy of contemplation but upheld country life as wholesome for the body, spirit, and the mind.

The landscape as a powerful vehicle of conception and as a dominant shaping force in Bucks County's cultural history can be traced to William Penn's vision in settling the region. Penn understood how the landscape could be used both as a vehicle of contemplation and as a deliverer of experience to entice settlers to his colony. The values of rural living and of the country as the "philosopher's garden and library" were central elements of his vision for settling Pennsylvania, a vision that identified the rural landscape as a rich resource for material and spiritual needs that was capable of changing the way individuals viewed the potential of their lives:

> The Country Life is to be preferr'd; for there we see the Works of God; but in Cities little else but the Works of Men: And the one makes a better Subject for our Contemplation than the other. . . . The Country is both the Philosopher's Garden and his Library, in which he Reads and Contemplates the Power, Wisdom and Goodness of God.[7]
>
> Love Labor: For if thou dost not want it for Food, thou mayest for Physick. It is wholesome for thy Body, and good for thy Mind. It prevents the Fruits of Idleness, which many times comes of nothing to do, and leads too many to do what is worse than nothing. A Garden, an Elaboratory, a Work-house, Improvements and Breeding, are pleasant and Profitable Diversions to the Idle and Ingenious: For here they miss Ill Company, and converse with Nature and Art; whose Variety are equally grateful and instructing; and preserve a good Constitution of Body and Mind.[8]

Nonetheless, the Quaker values of rural living and a plain style of life devoted to physical labor and useful work were not values that provided strong support for the pursuit or patronage of the fine arts among Bucks County's early, predominantly Quaker, settlers in the eighteenth and early nineteenth centuries. Early delineators of the Delaware Valley landscape during the eighteenth and early nineteenth centuries were in fact predominantly European rather than native-born artists. Bucks County Quaker minister and painter Edward Hicks (1780–1849) managed to pursue his art by restricting his technique to a simple, flat style of painting that could be associated with sign and related trade painting and by focusing his subject matter on ideas and messages acceptable to most Quakers.[9]

Although the Quakers were scornful of visual arts that functioned solely to please the senses, the evolving beliefs of the Hicksite Friends, who placed special emphasis on the Inward Light and on waiting for a direct experience from God, provided a foundation for the subsequent acceptance of art during the late nineteenth century as an expressive activity rooted in sensibility and feeling. While Quaker values continued to exert influence on the art produced throughout the nineteenth century, their influence was tempered by 1850 when Philadelphia emerged as a center for clinical scientific study. As scientists explored the human body and its functional relationship to the environment, a topic of considerable interest was the process by which animals and humans adapted to their environment. The proponents of neo-Lamarckian evolutionary thought, who attributed change within a species and the progress of society to the organism's successful adaptation to its environment, included Philadelphia paleontologist Edward Drinker Cope, who theorized that a society's progress was limited when its members were no longer actively engaged in the struggle for existence. Within this scientific environment, Philadelphia artist Thomas Eakins (1844–1916) became interested in the visible and invisible mechanisms that govern bodies in movement and expression as well as the vital organizing principles that determine the general forms of nature. As director of Philadelphia's Pennsylvania Academy of the Fine Arts from 1882 until 1886,

Eakins oriented the school's course of study to focus on the nude human figure and utilized progressive teaching methods that included exhaustive analyses of anatomy, perspective, motion, and perception.

The Pennsylvania Academy exerted increasing influence on regional artists during the nineteenth century, and Bucks County Quaker artists Thomas Hicks (1823–1890) and Jonathan K. Trego (1817–1901) were among these artists. After completing studies at the Pennsylvania Academy and the National Academy of Design, Hicks embarked on a grand tour of Europe and then returned to New York to produce portraits of celebrated literary, social, and political figures. While Jonathan Trego may have studied with Thomas Sully when he lived in Philadelphia and certainly participated in annual Pennsylvania Academy exhibitions from 1852 through 1868, his major patrons were prosperous Bucks County Quaker farmers and judges who wanted their diligently acquired prosperity and useful occupations to be expressed in a manner that reflected their plain style of life (*Smith Trego*, ca. 1840; pl. 82; and *Anna Phillips Trego*, ca. 1840; pl. 83).

Like Thomas Hicks, Martin Johnson Heade (1819–1904) apprenticed with Edward Hicks and traveled to England and the Continent during the 1840s. Although he never resided in Bucks County after his youth, he maintained strong ties with his family. His tropical landscapes, seascapes, paintings of marshes, and still lifes are highly sought after today, yet during his lifetime Heade was not a highly celebrated artist. The landscape was also pursued by Thomas Otter (1832–1890), a graduate of the Pennsylvania Academy, who moved to Bucks County after the Civil War. He garnered acclaim with his iconic painting *On the Road*, which associated westward expansion with the progress of the nation. His 1875 *The Palisades at Nockamixon* (pl. 66) documents the presence of the timber industry and disappearance of the wilderness in the region along the Delaware River in northern Bucks County. Another graduate of the Pennsylvania Academy was Jonathan Trego's son William B. T. Trego (1859–1909), who won critical renown for his action-packed Civil War scenes that featured horses galloping head-on (*Civil War Battle Scene,* 1887; pl. 35). A student of Thomas Eakins, Trego would certainly have known of his teacher's interest in modeling the movement of horses after Eadweard Muybridge's groundbreaking photographs of horses in motion. As a student at the academy in 1883, Trego would have been able to attend Muybridge's lecture "The Romance and Reality of Animals in Motion," in which the British photographer used a projecting zoetrope to show his photographs of animal locomotion.[10]

Other artists like Edward W. Redfield (1869–1965) and Daniel Garber (1880–1958) enrolled in the Pennsylvania Academy and learned first-hand, either from Eakins or his successor Thomas Anshutz, how to capture the solid sculptural mass of the figure. Eakins and Anshutz viewed art as fundamentally an expressive activity rooted in man's sensibility and feeling, and they stressed close observation and personal experience as essential to the artist's subtle depiction of nature's evanescent effects. As early as 1891 Robert Vonnoh joined the academy faculty and introduced the impressionist "French style of painting" to his students. From 1896 until 1909 William Merritt Chase, Henry McCarter, and Hugh Breckenridge taught their students at the academy about new Parisian styles of painting, encouraging artistic autonomy and experimentation. In 1898 Anshutz and Hugh Breckenridge established the Darby Summer Art School in Darby and subsequently in Fort Washington, Pennsylvania, where students like Daniel Garber could study plein air landscape painting.

When an economic depression disrupted the American economy in the 1890s, urban artists and craftsmen like painter Edward W. Redfield found refuge in the Bucks County countryside, settling there not just for the beauty of the physical landscape but because they could make a living from the land and still have the freedom to work creatively as they saw fit. Most of the New Hope painters, like the French impressionists of the 1870s, painted outdoors in direct contact

with the landscape. Their interest in capturing the ephemeral effects of natural phenomena evolved partially in response to new theories of perception and positivist doctrine that emphasized immediate personal experience as the starting point of all knowledge. The vigorous, direct style of many of the New Hope painters was likewise shaped by the influence of the Pennsylvania Academy on regional artists.

A vibrant art colony did not develop in the Bucks County region until the opening decade of the twentieth century, when the New Hope school of painters, also known as the Pennsylvania impressionists, attracted students and young artists to the area and made Bucks County the home of a nationally recognized style of landscape painting. By 1916 these artists had established a national reputation for their landscapes of the native environment. The group included artists William Langson Lathrop, Edward W. Redfield, Daniel Garber, Morgan Colt, Rae Sloan Bredin, Charles Rosen, Robert Spencer, and Walter Elmer Schofield. Referring to their work as America's first truly national expression, critic Guy Pène du Bois (1884–1958) described the Pennsylvania painters as vigorous men of the soil, battling the turbulent powers of nature, whose powerful landscapes emanated from a sensibility developed by their intimate encounters with nature.[11] As Pène du Bois reasoned, living in the country built character and offered opportunities for intense experience and bodily testing. His celebration of the New Hope artists' strong work ethic and direct engagement with the native soil connected with the ideals of many Americans who were apprehensive about the impact of urban mechanization on the creative spirit of individuals as the nation was undergoing a profound transition from a predominantly agrarian society to an industrial world power.

Modernist painters began to settle in the New Hope area in the teens and twenties, but modernist art did not gain momentum locally until the mid-twenties, when painter C. F. Ramsey established New Hope's first art gallery, the Blue Mask, which became a center for modernist art. By the

1930s New Hope had attracted painters Lloyd Ney, R.A.D. Miller, Ralston Crawford, Henry Baker, Adolphe Blondheim, Robert Hogue, Charles Evans, B.J.O. Nordfeldt, Lee Gatch, Elsie Driggs, Peter Keenan, and Louis Stone. Influenced by the innovations of the European avant-garde, the New Hope painters experimented with such modernist trends as cubism, futurism, surrealism, biomorphism, synchronism, precisionism, expressionism, and neoplasticism. Working with expressive color, abstract forms, and modern concepts of creative design, C. F. Ramsey, Louis Stone, and Charles Evans formed the Cooperative Painting Project in 1938, an experimental group that took turns and worked jointly to produce single works of nonobjective art. The Cooperative Painting Project took its cues from the improvisational style of jazz and the Quaker methods of consensus and association, and its members produced a number of innovative collective works during its two-year lifespan.[12] Creating work that grappled with new modes of understanding space, time, the past, the complex interior life of man, and the impact of the machine age on society, the New Hope modernist movement thrived well into the 1950s.

At the same time that the Pennsylvania impressionists were ascending to national recognition, Henry Chapman Mercer was active in Doylestown, building the Mercer Museum to house his collection of preindustrial American artifacts and the Moravian Pottery and Tile Works to revive interest in handcrafts. Both the Pennsylvania impressionist group and the Mercer tool museum and tile factory developed out of the strong currents of the late-nineteenth-century Arts and Crafts movement, which arose in response to industrialization's impact on the American scene, on its environment, on its rhythms of life and work, and on how objects were made. Daniel Garber's eleven-by-twenty-two-foot mural *A Wooded Watershed* (1926; pl. 36), commissioned by the Commonwealth of Pennsylvania and painted for the Pennsylvania Building's natural resources exhibition at the Philadelphia Sesquicentennial, is a powerful expression of an

aesthetic that celebrated the regenerative powers of the simple life. The mural depicts a primeval wilderness scene inhabited only by deer with shimmering light reflected on the trees and rock faces, elements that were being featured, ironically enough, in the Pennsylvania exhibition as prime raw materials destined for the state's industries. This remarkable painting later was moved to the forestry school at Pennsylvania State University in Mont Alto. Decades later, with the assistance from a Commonwealth of Pennsylvania legislative initiative grant awarded by former senator H. Craig Lewis, the Michener acquired the mural in 1994.

The Arts and Crafts movement in Bucks County at the turn of the twentieth century led to a revival of interest in handcraftsmanship. While the movement included artists of varying convictions, many craft leaders idealized the simple life of a preindustrial past and embraced the concept of integrating art into everyday life. Using indigenous materials and native craft traditions, artists began producing decorative objects for the home that were simple in form and functional in design. As a depression rocked the American economy in the 1890s and unemployment in the nation's cities reached 35 percent, many city dwellers retreated to the country to embrace the simple life and the moral work ethic of the subsistence farmer and craftsman as a path to a better life. Bucks County became a center for the production of handcarved frames by Frederick William Harer (pl. 3) and Bernard "Ben" Badura (pl. 56); handcrafted wooden and wrought-iron furnishings by Morgan Colt in his Gothic Shop at Phillips' Mill; and stained glass by George W. Sotter, produced in his Holicong glass studio and incorporating Gothic, Arts and Crafts, and medieval motifs. Woodworker George Nakashima settled in New Hope in the 1940s, where he established a studio and a reputation as a leading member of the first generation of American studio furniture makers. Carefully selecting timbers, Nakashima designed each piece around the distinctive properties of the wood. Reacting against post–World War II factory-made furniture, such Bucks County craftsmen as Phillip Lloyd Powell, Paul Evans, and Robert Whitley began producing unique, custom-designed functional furniture that blurred the traditional boundaries between craft, sculpture, and design. As early as the 1970s, craftsperson and sculptor Mark Sfirri began experimenting with multiaxis turnings to produce furniture and, subsequently, eccentrically turned wall sculptures.

The flip side of expressing the vital energy of a specific person, place, or thing is the exploration of the fluid boundaries of time and space and the shifting identity of people, objects, and places. In the past twenty-five years, the growth of digital technologies, new media, mass visual culture, and multiculturalism has offered artists like Catherine Jansen, David Graham, and Peter Rose new modes of conceptualizing and creating visual art while also spurring interest in new ways of perceiving and thinking about physical and cultural environments. While some contemporary artists, like Robert Dodge, have adopted details from architecture and design to raise philosophical questions about the importance of originality, others like Alan Magee have focused on large-scale realist paintings of commonplace objects to show the innate power still resident in a familiar object. Still others like Mavis Smith, Paul Keene, and Rob Evans employ figurative and naturalistic styles to create alternative worlds or dreamlike scenes or to imbue man and nature with diffused presences as they explore the complexities of identity, the structure of time, and the psychic dimensions of a place.

BUILDING PARTNERSHIPS: FROM WISH LISTS TO INCLUSIVE PROCESSES

During its first decade, the Michener Art Museum built its permanent collection by partnering with artists, artists' families, community organizations and businesses, and individual donors. In 1994 the museum sponsored a competition and invited woodworkers from the Mid-Atlantic region to submit proposals for a bench. Robert Whitley, who had earned a national reputation for his workmanship in the contemporary studio furniture movement of the seventies and eighties,

won the competition with his proposal for a bench in his signature Throne series. The museum subsequently acquired the bench.

During the same period, the museum acquired a collection of Harry Leith-Ross's conté crayon drawings (*Early Spring, New Hope Area*, n.d.; pl. 39; and *Factory Fire, Leiden, Holland*, 1965; pl. 38) as a gift from his wife, Emily, as well as George W. Sotter's dramatic cloud-filled landscape painting, *Buckingham Mountain*, given by Charles W. Hargens Jr. In 1994 an anonymous donor established a purchase fund for acquisitions, and with a corporate match by Johnson & Johnson, the museum began a more active collecting strategy, purchasing William B. T. Trego's *Civil War Battle Scene* (1887; pl. 35) and Ben Solowey's portrait of his wife *Rae Seated (Green Dress)* (1935; pl. 27), as well as work by such modernist and contemporary artists as Lee Gatch (*Eastern Eagle*, 1958; pl. 42), Paul F. Keene (*Street Quartet*, 1990), Alan Goldstein (*Upriver from Lumberville Walking Bridge II*, ca. 1981; pl. 37), Robert Dodge (*Shutters Reapportioned*, 1995; and *Slanted Lintel*, 1995), and Selma Bortner (*Aida and the Serpent*, 1990). The purchase fund was also used to acquire and expand significant holdings of contemporary photographs by David Graham, Michael Smith (*Near Frenchtown, New Jersey*, 1973; pl. 68), and Jack Rosen (*George Nakashima*, 1973; pl. 43). The Bortner, Dodge, and Graham works appeared in the museum's first Bucks County Invitational exhibit (1997) and subsequently were purchased for the museum's permanent collection.

In 1997 the Michener purchased one of its most significant nineteenth-century holdings: Thomas Hicks's portrait of his older cousin Edward Hicks (ca. 1850–52; pl. 25), painted shortly after the elder man's death in 1849. The portrait, one of three versions that Thomas painted, depicts Edward at work on one of his *Peaceable Kingdom* paintings. Thomas likely created this version to honor Edward's ingenuity in focusing his *Peaceable Kingdom* series on subject matter that contained ideas and messages acceptable to the evolving aesthetic of Hicksite Quakers.[13]

The acquisition was made possible through the generosity of individuals and foundations in the community as well as members of the Newtown Friends Meeting.

To celebrate the seventy-fifth anniversary of the Doylestown Hospital, the museum commissioned photographer Edmund Eckstein to create a series of images of Doylestown Hospital patients and staff. These photographs were acquired for the permanent collection and formed the basis of a commemorative exhibition held in 1998. That same year the Michener acquired Joseph T. Pearson's prize-winning portrait of his daughters *The Twins: Virginia and Jane* (1917; pl. 29), which earned him gold medals from the 1917 Pennsylvania Academy Annual Exhibition and the 1926 Philadelphia Sesquicentennial. The museum also augmented its collection of Daniel Garber landscape and figure sketches donated in 1993 by Dana Garber Applestein with six additional figure sketches gifted by Madelaine B. Garber (*Little Girl Knitting*, 1918; pl. 28; *Portrait of Frank Baisden*, ca. 1923; pl. 31).

The following year the Michener celebrated its first decade with an exhibition of forty works from the collection. The exhibition opened with the unveiling of a major Edward W. Redfield acquisition, made possible through funds secured by local residents and the Redfield family: *The Burning of Center Bridge* (1923; pl. 40), a dramatic night scene depicting the 1923 fire that destroyed the bridge connecting Center Bridge, Pennsylvania, with Stockton, New Jersey. Although Redfield observed the fiery scene, taking notes on an envelope as the fire raged, he departed from his practice of painting a landscape *en plein air* and waited to re-create the scene in his studio. Within two days Redfield created this canvas, which captures the heroic efforts of firemen trying to extinguish the blaze as spectators stand by helplessly watching the burning wooden structure glow against a black sky filled with plumes of smoke. The destruction of the region's oldest Delaware River covered bridge was a significant event. News of the incident appeared in the *Washington Post*[14] and in the headlines of the local

Bucks County Intelligencer, which recounted the drama of twenty-five firemen falling into the river as they fought the fire while "the banks of the river were lined with a crowd aggregating thousands of spectators."[15]

When Marguerite and H. F. "Gerry" Lenfest placed fifty-nine paintings in trust to the Michener Art Museum in 1999, their promised gift, which was converted to an outright gift in 2005, transformed the museum from a young institution striving to build a collection into an institution that functions as an exhibition and study center of Pennsylvania impressionism. The museum renovated its Putman Smith Gallery to house the collection, which includes noteworthy examples of the New Hope school of painters such as William Langson Lathrop's *Chilmark Moor, Martha's Vineyard* (1930; pl. 54), Edward W. Redfield's *The Trout Brook* (ca. 1916; pl. 47), Daniel Garber's *Springtime in the Village* (1917; pl. 52), George Sotter's *Brace's Cove* (n.d.; pl. 55) and *The Windybush Valley* (1939; pl. 56), Robert Spencer's *A Gray Day* (1912; pl. 50), and Charles Rosen's *Opalescent Morning* (ca. 1909; pl. 53). The Lenfest gift included a $3 million dollar endowment to care for the collection and establish the position of curator of collections, a position filled in 2001 by Constance Kimmerle. The Lenfest Collection enhanced the museum's collecting, research, and educational functions at the most fundamental levels and allowed the museum to begin shaping its Pennsylvania impressionist collection. The gift also provides support for exhibitions and publications, including a major survey and its accompanying publication[16] of Pennsylvania impressionism organized by senior curator Brian Peterson, which toured the United States, as well as retrospective exhibitions and monographs on Bucks County frame makers in addition to painters Edward W. Redfield, Robert Spencer, Harry Leith-Ross, and Charles Rosen.

In September 2000 the museum opened the Patricia D. Pfundt Sculpture Garden. Nine works by sculptors Eric Berg, Allan Houser, Doug Hyde, Jo Jenks, Barry Johnston, Masami Kodama (*Six Triangles,* 1966; pl. 6), Barbara Lekberg (*Sea*

Wind II, 1998; pl. 33), and Greg Wyatt were displayed in an outdoor setting designed to suggest the geography of the Bucks County landscape. With the assistance of the Friends of Selma Burke, the Michener initiated a project to cast in bronze Burke's relief sculpture *Together* (1975, cast 2001; pl. 65) for display in the garden. In that same year the museum organized its Fourth Bucks County Invitational, which included Emmet Gowin's photograph *Edith, Danville* (1970, printed 2000). The exhibition became the occasion for the museum's first purchase of work by the renowned photographer. Four years later the museum augmented its photography collection with the purchase of nine silver gelatin prints that included selections from Gowin's early family portrait series (*Nancy, Danville*, 1969; pl. 85) as well as Gowin's later aerial images of the American West.

Over the next few years, the Michener strengthened its holdings of work by contemporary artists, acquiring through gifts, trust agreements, and purchases such works as Alan Magee's giclée prints of imaginary faces of hybrid creatures bearing sutures, scratch marks, and haunting facial expressions (*Silence* and *Wound*, 1995, printed 2004; pl. 80); a large-scale, vigorous pure abstraction by Philadelphia artist James Lueders (*Untitled*, 1973; pl. 76); an expansive landscape from Diane Burko's Volcano series (*Vulcano from the Air*, 2001; pl. 67); a surreal landscape by Rob Evans, addressing the life cycle of his personal associations to his grandmother's home (*Cicada*, 1998–2000; pl. 72); a large-scale drawing of trees by Emily Brown, focusing on the dynamic rhythms and forms of nature (*Fond Farewell*, 2002; pl. 99); and Catherine Jansen's novel soft sculpture environment *The Blue Room* (1970; pl. 115). The museum continued to build its contemporary sculpture collection with works that showcase the innovative poured bronze technique of Isaac Witkin (*Waif's Anchors*, 1986; pl. 91), as well as Arlene Love's use of polyester resins in sculpture (*Maddy at 18*, 1976; pl. 103). Harry Gordon's *Flying K,* Kevin Forest's *Sailing by the Moon,* Mark Pettegrow's *Mariposa,* and Joe Mooney's *Phoenix* were acquired from the

museum's outdoor sculpture exhibition program spearheaded by Brian Peterson. The dual commitment to support contemporary artists and civic causes was a driving force behind the purchase of two works addressing the issue of domestic violence: Selma Bortner's collograph *This Is How I Feel When You Hollar at Me* (2002) and Marlene Miller's charcoal drawing *If I Can't Have You No One Will* (2001; pl. 58) were selected from the Michener's 2002 exhibition *A Celebration of Voices: The Twenty-fifth Anniversary of A Woman's Place,* which honored the nationally acclaimed Bucks County organization that works on behalf of abused women and children. The museum also added to its collection of modernist work Charles Ward's magical spring landscape, *Goldie Peacock's House* (1935; pl. 62).

The formation of the Janus Society in 2002 and the establishment of the Beveridge Moore and Henry Morof Collections Care and Acquisitions Endowment in 2005 enabled the Michener to expand its permanent collection with both breadth and quality. Janus Society donors provide funds for permanent collection acquisitions. Led by collections committee chairman William Mandel, the Janus Society has funded the purchase of Rae Sloan Bredin's lush summer canal scene *After the Rain* (1913; pl. 105); Randall Exon's evocative *Beach House* (2002; pl. 111); Nelson Shanks's bust-length rear-view portrait of a young subject (*Pigtails*, 2004; pl. 89); and Alan Magee's monumental painting of beach stones (*Countermeasure*, 2004; pl. 93). The Bette and G. Nelson Pfundt Photography Endowment has enabled the Michener to broaden and refine its contemporary photography collection to include work by Ricardo Barros (*Isaac Witkin*, 1996; pl. 84), H. Scott Heist (*Alexander Calder and White Cascades*, 1976; pl. 79), Edmund Eckstein (*Basic Training, Fort Jackson South Carolina* and *May Day Rally [Philadelphia, May 1969],* printed 2007; pl. 87 and 86), Michael Becotte (*Construction #339*, 2003; pl. 88), Stephen Guion Williams (*Sunrise, Chosen Land*, 1972; pl. 112), and Suzanne Opton (*Soldier: Benson—368 Days in Iraq*, 2005; pl. 95).

In 2004 the Michener unveiled the newly acquired work *Study for New London Facets* (1940; pl. 59) by New Hope modernist Lloyd Ney. A rare example of an abstract work that was commissioned by the United States Treasury Department's Section of Painting and Sculpture as part of its Depression-era post office mural program, this four-panel mural painted for the New London, Ohio, post office dynamically narrates the forces of energy and activity that molded the city's history through time and space.

Recently the museum has acquired modernist work by Charles Rosen (*Quarry and Crusher*, ca. early 1930s; pl.108) and Elsie Driggs (*Moonstruck Goat*, 1957). These acquisitions coincided with retrospective exhibitions and monographs produced by senior curator Brian Peterson and curator of collections Constance Kimmerle that explored these artists' contributions to American modernism. With the purchase in 2007 of Peter Rose's *Rotary Almanac* (2000) and *Geosophist's Tears* (2002), the museum broadened its contemporary holdings to include the experience of landscape as it is conveyed through cinematic media.

NEW DIRECTIONS

Since 1993 visitors to the museum have experienced the ambiance of a traditional Japanese-style room in the *George Nakashima Memorial Reading Room* designed by Mira Nakashima-Yarnall, daughter of George Nakashima. The Michener Art Museum has recently expanded its collection of Bucks County furniture with a desk and side chair with art deco–inspired ornamental motifs by Frederick W. Harer (ca. 1930s; pl. 113), as well as work from the American studio furniture movement, such as Phillip Lloyd Powell's carved and sculpted fireplace from his mid-fifties New Hope studio (ca. 1956–58; pl. 81); a Robert Whitley desk and armchair, representing two of his finest efforts from his signature Throne series (1999; pl. 114); and chairs from Paul Evans's corrugated cardboard furniture line (1976), designed for transient people who "fall in love in the morning, buy furniture in the afternoon, and move in together in the evening." [17]

In 2008 Mira Nakshima-Yarnall and Kevin Nakashima chose the Michener as the principal repository for the archival collection of their father, George Nakashima. This gift enables the Michener to become a center of research for one of the most significant figures in the American studio furniture movement.

The Michener revised its mission statement in 2007 to expand its collecting scope to include American art while still preserving the focus on art of the Bucks County region. The John Horton Collection is an example of the Michener's growing in new areas while building on its holdings of art with political and social content. John Horton dedicated his life and work to civic causes. With encouragement from New York art dealer Samuel Rosenfeld, he began collecting art in the 1980s that focused on the ties of people to their community, on the values of hard work, and on injustices and the human condition. The Horton Collection, a gift of John Horton, includes work by artists who figured prominently in the American Scene and social realist movements of the Depression era, such as William Gropper, William Schwartz (*Come to Me All Ye That Are Heavy Laden,* 1934; pl. 107), Guy Pène du Bois (*In the Courtroom*, n.d.; pl. 97), Eugene Higgins (*A Connecticut Ploughman,* n.d.; pl. 106), Robert Gwathmey (*End of Day*, 1943; pl. 90), and Ben Shahn (*Study for Riker's Island Mural*, ca.1934; pl. 98).

The museum's library and archives will soon be housed in a space currently used for changing exhibitions. The archival collections include material relating to the institution's history, the cultural history of the region, and the artists represented in the museum's permanent collection, and they enhance the collecting, research, and public program activities of the museum. Recent acquisitions include collections that are rich resources for scholarship into the life and work of William Langson Lathrop, George Sotter, and Phillip Lloyd Powell.

As the Michener Art Museum enters its third decade, we of the museum's staff and board continue to reassess the value judgments and criteria behind our activities, mindful that the same system of values behind our selection of objects for the collection also operates when we subject works to interpretation and decide how collections will be managed. James Michener's perceptive understanding of the role of museums and their collections is as important today as it was thirty years ago. Being acutely aware of the evolving tastes and dynamic pressures that underlay museums' collecting, interpretation, and preservation activities, he would likely advise museum keepers today to live with more uncertainty and avoid representing their knowledge as definitive. Our ultimate challenge is to be mindful stewards yet responsive to the need to deliver engaging, meaningful experiences.

NOTES

1. National Endowment for the Arts, 1997 Survey of Public Participation in the Arts (Washington, DC: National Endowment for the Arts, 1998), quoted in Bonnie Pitman, "Muses, Museums, and Memories," *Daedalus, Proceedings of the American Academy of Arts and Sciences* 128, no. 3 (summer 1999): 1.

2. "The Collector: An Informal Memoir," *The James A. Michener Collection: Twentieth-Century American Painting* (Austin: University of Texas at Austin, 1977), xvi–xvii.

3. Ibid., xviii.

4. Herman Silverman, "History of the James A. Michener Art Center," *Inaugural Exhibition of Twentieth-Century American Art* (Doylestown, PA: James A. Michener Art Center of Bucks County, 1988), ix. Published in conjunction with *Inaugural Exhibition of Twentieth-Century American Art*, Doylestown, PA, September 15 through May 28, 1988.

5. The collection would be further enriched during the nineties with additional donations from the artist's wife.

6. Board of trustees minutes, James A. Michener Art Museum, January 21, 1991.

7. William Penn, "A Country Life," in *Some Fruits of Solitude in Reflections and Maxims,* part 1 (London: Headley Brothers: 1693; reprinted 1905), 62.

8. Penn, "Industry," *Some Fruits of Solitude*, 35–36.

9. Carolyn J. Weekley, "Edward Hicks: Quaker Artist and Minister," *Quaker Aesthetics: Reflections on a Quaker Ethic in American Design and Consumption*, ed. Emma Jones Lapsansky and Anne A. Verplanck (Philadelphia: University of Pennsylvania Press, 2003), 212–234.

10. Muybridge letters to George Corliss, February 3, 1883, and February 6, 1883, Archives of the Pennsylvania Academy of the Fine Arts.

11. Guy Pène du Bois, "The Boston Group of Painters: An Essay on Nationalism in Art," *Arts and Decoration* 5, no. 12 (October 1915): 457, 459.

12. For more discussion of the Cooperative Painting Project experiment, see Roy Pedersen's essay on "The New Hope Modernists," in *New Hope Modernists 1917–1950* (New Hope, PA: New Hope Modernist Project, 1991), 8–14.

13. The Hicksites, who became increasingly liberal over time, placed special emphasis on the Inward Light. Believing in waiting for a direct experience from God more than finding it in the Bible, they broke away from the mainstream Quaker movement in 1827.

14. "Fifteen Fall with Bridge on Fire," *Washington Post*, July 23, 1923.

15. "Twenty-five Firemen Dropped to River When Bolt Fired Centre Bridge-Stockton Bridge," *Bucks County Intelligencer,* July 26, 1923.

16. Brian H. Peterson, William H. Gerdts, and Sylvia Yount, *Pennsylvania Impressionism* (Doylestown, PA: James A. Michener Art Museum; Philadelphia: University of Pennsylvania Press, 2002).

17. Paul Evans quoted in Josephine Marcotty, "See the Apartment from These Seats," *Dayton Daily News*, November 26, 1978, news clipping, James A. Michener Art Museum Archives.

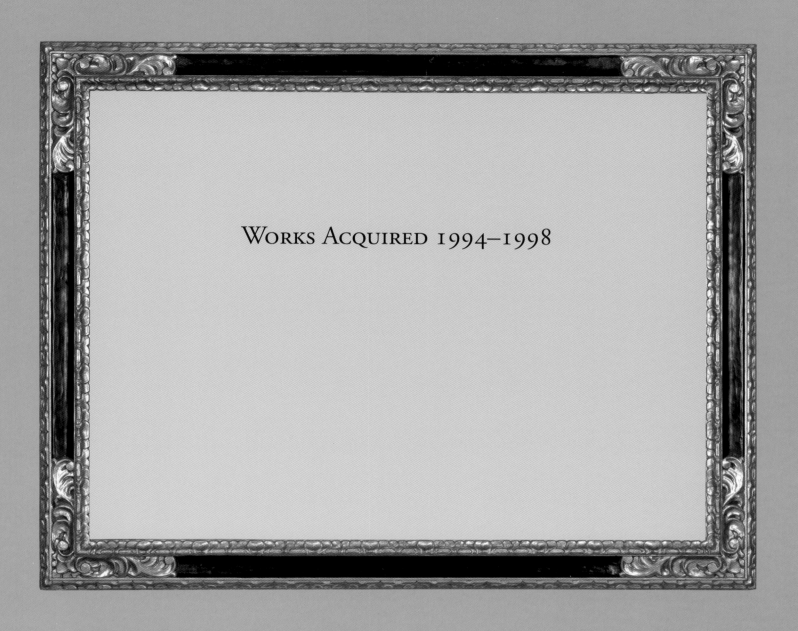

Works Acquired 1994–1998

PORTRAIT OF EDWARD HICKS BY THOMAS HICKS, ACQUIRED 1997

Conversations with Bruce Katsiff

The portrait of Edward Hicks by his younger cousin, Thomas Hicks, was another important addition to the museum's collection. It is actually one of three portraits of Edward Hicks done by Thomas, but the only one that was done after Edward's death. The other two works are in the collections of the Abby Aldrich Rockefeller Folk Art Museum and the National Portrait Gallery.

The picture has always offered me some insight into Edward Hicks's personality. Hicks was critical of his own identity as a painter. He described painting as a trifling art, of little significance. In his own writing Hicks talked about his hope that he would be remembered as a preacher, but what is intriguing about this picture is that he is posed as a painter. While the Bible is included in the portrait, it is in the background and is clearly subservient to the presentation of Edward Hicks as an artist.

The painting came to our attention through the recommendation of two local dealers who have always supported folk art in America, Ed Hild and Patrick Bell. They called me one day to say that a New York gallery was showing a work by Thomas Hicks and they were representing a private collector who owned the picture. Both thought it would be a terrific addition to the Michener's collection. I was in complete agreement. All that was needed were the resources to acquire it.

We first turned to members of the Quaker community in the Newtown area and spoke with representatives of the Newtown Friends Meeting. With the help of Kingdon Swayne, a former colleague from my college days, we made the argument that it would be important for this picture to remain in Bucks County and be represented in the Michener collection. Swayne made many introductions for us, and we were able to find a range of individuals who supported this effort and helped us to purchase the painting. Among the final donors for its acquisition were Hild and Bell, who contributed their finder's fee that they received from the gallery.

From a recorded conversation with
***Kristy Krivitsky**, November 4, 2008*

25
THOMAS HICKS (1823–1890)
Portrait of Edward Hicks ca. 1850–52
oil on canvas, 36⅛ x 29⅛ inches
James A. Michener Art Museum
Museum purchase funded by Eleanor K. Denoon, The Bella S. and Benjamin H. Garb Foundation Inc., Mr. and Mrs. Kenneth Gemmill, George S. Hobensack Jr., Laurence D. Keller, William Mandel, Members of Newtown Friends Meeting, Olde Hope Antiques, Inc., Residents of Pennswood Village, Eleanor and Malcolm Polis, Ms. Leslie E. Skilton, Kingdon Swayne, and Anonymous Donors

26
DANIEL GARBER (1880–1958)
Garden Window 1946
etching and drypoint on paper, 11⅜ x 10¼ inches
James A. Michener Art Museum
Gift of Mrs. John Garber

27
BEN SOLOWEY (1900–1978)
Rae Seated (Green Dress) 1935
oil on canvas, 45 x 36 inches
James A. Michener Art Museum
Museum purchase funded by Anne and Joseph Gardocki

28
DANIEL GARBER (1880–1958)
Little Girl Knitting 1918
charcoal on laid paper, 23¼ x 18¼ inches
James A. Michener Art Museum
Gift of Madelaine B. Garber

29
JOSEPH T. PEARSON JR. (1876–1951)
The Twins: Virginia and Jane   1917
oil on canvas, 60 x 72 inches
James A. Michener Art Museum
Gift of Oliver Pearson

30
RICHARD KEMBLE (1932–2007)
Palenque 1974
color woodcut on paper, 29½ x 21½ inches
James A. Michener Art Museum
Gift of George F. Korn

31
DANIEL GARBER (1880–1958)
Portrait of Frank Baisden ca. 1923
charcoal on laid paper, 23¼ x 17¾ inches
James A. Michener Art Museum
Gift of Madelaine B. Garber

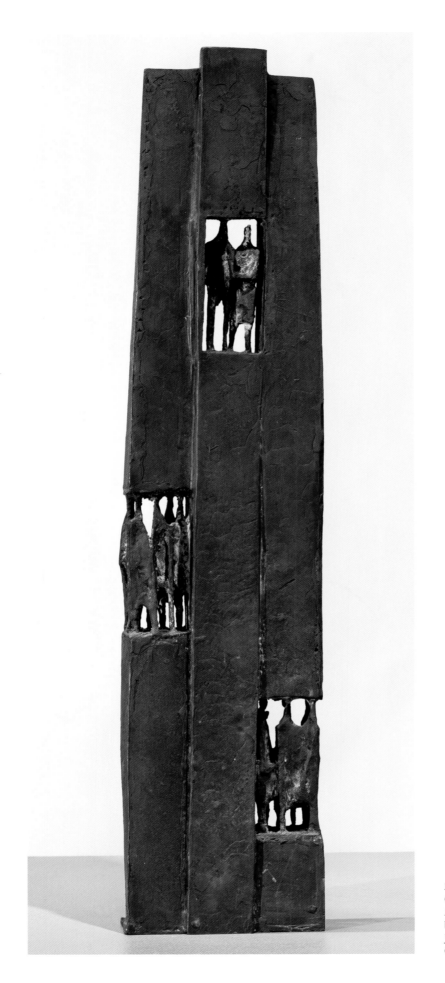

32
GERD UTESCHER (1912–1983)
Elevators 1971
bronze, 27 x 5¾ x 2 inches
James A. Michener Art Museum
Gift of Anne D. Utescher

33
BARBARA LEKBERG (b. 1925)
Sea Wind II 1998
bronze, 45 x 30 x 15 inches
James A. Michener Art Museum
Museum purchase funded by a grant
from the Florsheim Art Fund

35
WILLIAM B. T. TREGO (1859–1909)
Civil War Battle Scene 1887
oil on canvas, 19¼ x 29½ inches
James A. Michener Art Museum
Museum purchase funded by Anne and Joseph Gardocki

34
MAXIMILIAN VANKA (1889–1963)
Untitled (Miners, Pittsburgh) 1935
ink on paper, 25½ x 20 inches
James A. Michener Art Museum
Gift of Margaret Vanka Brasko

36
DANIEL GARBER (1880–1958)
A Wooded Watershed 1926
oil on canvas, 129¼ x 257¼ inches
James A. Michener Art Museum
Acquired with a Legislative Initiative Grant
awarded by Senator H. Craig Lewis

A WOODED WATERSHED BY DANIEL GARBER, ACQUIRED 1994

Conversations with Bruce Katsiff

The Michener Art Endowment Challenge brought us many fine works of art, but perhaps one of the most interesting stories concerns the acquisition of Daniel Garber's *A Wooded Watershed.* Marjory Blubaugh, a librarian at the Mont Alto branch campus of the Pennsylvania State University, read a story about the Michener Art Endowment Challenge in her morning paper. She noticed that we were looking for work by the artist Daniel Garber. That name rang a bell, because she knew that an old Garber painting was in the campus auditorium. Marjory called me and left a message with my secretary. Needless to say, that is the kind of message you love to find on your desk! I promptly called Marjory, and she told me about the mural and wondered if we would be interested Well, we certainly were.

We were aware that Garber had done this mural, but knowledge of its whereabouts had been lost. In fact, Garber's family had searched for the mural, but they were under the impression that it was on the main campus of Penn State and had been unable to find it. Dana Applestein (Garber's granddaughter), Carolyn Smith (the then-president of the museum's board), and I decided to visit Mont Alto and take a closer look at the mural.

Before we went, we had a chance to do more research and learned that Garber had been commissioned to produce a mural to decorate the Pennsylvania pavilion for the Sesquicentennial Exposition, which was held in Philadelphia in 1926. Garber received a $3,000 commission for the work, and he painted it in six weeks. It was twenty-two feet across, eleven feet high, in a half-moon shape, and was installed in the building above a doorway. When the sesquicentennial closed, it was decided that the mural should go to a new forestry school that was opening in Mont Alto. Forestry was a major industry in Pennsylvania in the 1920s, and it seemed appropriate for the work to be housed there. Under Garber's supervision the mural was installed at the back of the school's auditorium, but there was a small problem—the mural was twenty-two feet wide while the auditorium was only nineteen feet wide.

We arrived at Mont Alto and went to see Marjory in the library. She took us over to the auditorium. When we walked into the space, the stage was in front of us and the curtains were pulled. We could barely see the painting, but there were some stage lights around, so I immediately took one of those lights and plugged it in, turned it on, and shined it on the mural. I must say that in that instant I knew it was a spectacular piece and somehow we had to get it, even though its condition was atrocious. There were nineteen rips in the canvas. The corners were not to be seen, and we didn't know if they had been cut off.

The next problem was figuring out how to acquire the mural. We began negotiations with the president of the Mont Alto campus to see if they would transfer ownership to the Michener and we would undertake the conservation on the work. We had conservators visit and examine it, got estimates on what the conservation would cost, talked to the folks familiar with Garber's work, and then began the process of negotiating the acquisition itself. Our idea was that we would endow a scholarship at Mont Alto in Garber's name to help a needy student in exchange for their transferring ownership of the painting to the Michener.

We eventually came to an agreement, and the next project was to remove, preserve, and install the work at the museum. To do all of this was going to require a great deal of money, which was going to be a challenge, but at that point another angel stepped forward to help us. That person was Craig Lewis. Lewis was then a state senator in the Pennsylvania state legislature. We told Craig about this piece of Pennsylvania history, where it was, what terrible condition it was in, and our desire to bring it back to life and make it a centerpiece of the Michener. Craig believed in the importance of this project and was able to get us a legislative initiative grant that enabled us to pay for the restoration work.

It was a great day when we arrived with our conservators and began to remove the mural from the wall. Much to our joy we discovered that the corners had not been cut but that Garber had folded them back. As we began to examine the canvas, it was also clear that while the canvas was filthy and had holes in it, it had suffered no light damage because it had been in the back of the auditorium. We had complete confidence that once it was cleaned and repaired, it would have the original vitality that it had when Garber first painted it. Another discovery we made was that Garber had decided not to varnish the canvas. While the varnish layer serves to protect a painting, it also makes future restoration extremely difficult because varnish tends to discolor and removing it is a major effort. Garber's decision not to varnish made our restoration work a little easier.

We hired Barbara Buckley, an extremely competent restorer, to do the restoration work. Barbara didn't have a studio large enough to work on the mural, so we had to rent a warehouse for the conservation. I said that it took Garber six weeks to paint the picture, but it took Barbara six months to bring it back to life. She removed every bit of dirt and grime, repaired all of the tears in the canvas, and flattened the work to eliminate the creases where it had been folded. She also built a new stretcher, and we moved the work to the Michener in a large trailer truck.

Then we met with another bit of good luck. Most of the museum is designed to accommodate moving a ten-foot object into the loading dock and up into the galleries, but we had built the Putman Smith Gallery in 1992 with a fourteen-foot-high ceiling and a fourteen-foot-high emergency exit just in case there would be a time when we needed to get a larger object into the space. Because we had that larger emergency exit, we were able to get the Garber mural through the door and into the gallery without having to remove a portion of the wall.

Acquiring, restoring, and installing the Garber mural is certainly one of the highlights of my career at the Michener. I think it will continue to be an important work that people will enjoy for many, many years in the future.

From a recorded conversation with
Kristy Krivitsky, *October 29, 2008*

37
ALAN GOLDSTEIN (b. 1938)
Upriver from Lumberville Walking Bridge II ca. 1981
oil on canvas, 65 x 96½ inches
James A. Michener Art Museum
Museum purchase funded by Anne and Joseph Gardocki

38
HARRY LEITH-ROSS (1886–1973)
Factory Fire, Leiden, Holland 1965
conté crayon on paper, 3 x 3¾ inches
James A. Michener Art Museum
Gift of Emily Leith-Ross

39
HARRY LEITH-ROSS (1886–1973)
Early Spring, New Hope Area n.d.
conté crayon on paper, 3¼ x 5 inches
James A. Michener Art Museum
Gift of Emily Leith-Ross

THE BURNING OF CENTER BRIDGE
BY EDWARD W. REDFIELD, ACQUIRED 1998

Conversations with Bruce Katsiff

Very often a family member will serve as the "keeper of the flame" who helps to build and maintain interest in the work of a deceased artist. Dorothy Redfield, the daughter-in-law of Edward Redfield, served in that role for the Redfield family. With the help of a niece, I was invited to visit Dorothy and see her collection of Redfield paintings and family artifacts. When we went to Dorothy's apartment, one of the first things that struck me was a grouping of three paintings made by Redfield. All three were of Center Bridge, which is the bridge that links the small town of Center Bridge, Pennsylvania, with Stockton, New Jersey. On the left was a painting of the covered wooden bridge that had been built there originally, in the middle was *The Burning of Center Bridge,* and on the right was a painting of the steel suspension bridge that was built after the fire. This was a powerful triptych, and one of my early thoughts was that I would love to have it in the Michener Museum.

When the museum was first founded, Dorothy was quite generous and gave the museum *Fleecydale Road,* which was one of the first Redfields in our collection. We eventually did a number of projects with her, and at some point I started to reveal that the museum would really love to acquire *The Burning of Center Bridge.*

40
EDWARD W. REDFIELD (1869–1965)
The Burning of Center Bridge   1923
oil on canvas, 50¼ x 56¼ inches
James A. Michener Art Museum
Acquired with funds secured by State Senator Joe Conti, and gifts
from Joseph and Anne Gardocki, and the Laurent Redfield Family

I always felt as though she was somewhat surprised by the choice, because it is obviously a different kind of picture by Redfield, but there are many interesting stories about the painting.

The story that we tell may be apocryphal, but Redfield was returning home from a visit with an artist friend in Philadelphia, and as he came down the river valley, he saw a fire. He was terrified because he thought his house was burning, as it stood directly next to Center Bridge. As he got to the bottom of the hill, he discovered that the bridge—not his home—was on fire, and he soon joined a crowd assembled to watch the firemen desperately try to put it out. As he stood there, his friend William Lathrop, the fellow artist, came up to him and said, "How'd you like to try and paint that picture?" Jumping to the challenge, Redfield made some sketches that evening and then, in his studio over the course of the next several days, painted two versions of *The Burning of Center Bridge.*

I have always felt that this work is one of the most important pieces in the museum's collection, because it represents the artistic heritage of the region and it's also a historic document about a dramatic event that occurred in the community. We were so pleased to have worked with Dorothy to acquire this painting.

From a recorded conversation
*with **Kristy Krivitsky**, October 29, 2008*

41
JOHN FULTON FOLINSBEE (1892–1972)
River Ice   1935
oil on canvas, 32¼ x 40 inches
James A. Michener Art Museum
Gift of the John Folinsbee Art Trust

42
LEE GATCH (1902–1968)
Eastern Eagle   1958
oil on canvas, 24½ x 33½ inches
James A. Michener Art Museum
Museum purchase funded by Anne and Joseph Gardocki

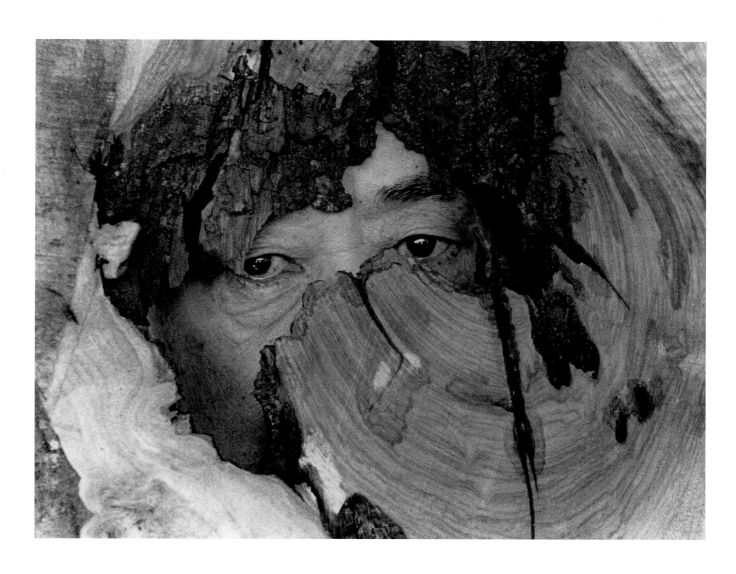

43
JACK ROSEN (1923–2006)
George Nakashima 1973
selenium toned print on paper, 7 x 9 inches
James A. Michener Art Museum
Museum purchase funded by Anne and Joseph Gardocki

44
TONY ROSATI (b. 1947)
Red Run   1995
monotype and watercolor on paper, 5⅞ x 8 inches
James A. Michener Art Museum
Gift of the artist

45
ROBERT DODGE (b. 1939)
Four Plans 1994
acrylic, gold leaf on wood, 19¼ x 37¼ inches
James A. Michener Art Museum
Museum purchase

This does not simplistically mean that an artist chooses to write about or depict only what is right before her eyes or within a several-mile radius of her home. Creative inspiration can derive from the energy of a network of other creative people, such as the visionaries whom early-twentieth-century American expatriates met in the salons of Paris. The history and culture of an area might spark creativity, as it did with the museum's namesake, James A. Michener (1907–1997). His stories about various corners of America and about certain lands abroad did not come about purely through research in a library's holdings. He felt the need to live in each area, sometimes for several years or longer, to absorb its rich and deeply held traditions before he could complete a manuscript.

But quite often it is the natural or man-made features of a region that speak decidedly to an artist's soul. The crashing of surf on rocky promontories along the Maine coast, the hot colors of the American Southwest, the cityscapes of the New York City skyline—these and infinitely more not only lure an artist into staying in their presence, but the locales themselves serve as a muse for the artist much as a particular model might inspire another painter or sculptor. Locality is especially important in an immediate sense for the landscape artist in the realist genres. But the fact is, the colors and light of a region, the climate and wildlife, the tree-covered mountains or vast flat expanses, the foliage and waterways—all conspire to influence and permeate even the most abstract artwork created in a particular place.

Bucks County as Flourishing Artist Haven

The Bucks County region has played host to a thriving succession of artists since European colonists settled in Pennsylvania. From Colonial times through the present era, increasing numbers of artists have chosen to establish their studios and homes around Bucks County. Many types of artists have felt this call: those trained in the major art academies and the self-taught; those who garnered national and international awards as well as those who labored in obscurity only to have their

work appreciated after death; artists who eagerly embraced an art colony that turned the eyes of the art world in their direction and those who worked in fierce solidarity yet with no less acclaim.

As art movements, genres, and styles have swept the art world, they all have been reflected to some extent in the work produced in Bucks County. Some artists have flown in the face of whatever prevailing mode held sway in their time. Yet these people and others of every stripe have flocked to this corner of eastern Pennsylvania, inspired by what they found. And this trend continues in contemporary times: artists can still be found dotting the Bucks County riverbanks and canal locks, perched behind their easels above quarries or on country lanes and town streets. Galleries and arts organizations proliferate to accommodate them.

The quality of creative activity in this rich and lengthy tradition—though by no means uniform—has ensured that a number of the region's artists have found their way into the annals of American art history. Bucks County is recognized around the country as a destination rich in art and art history.

The question is: what has drawn artists to the region? What have they discovered here to inspire them in such numbers and so consistently? The answers can be found by taking a look at the varied art created in the area, in particular the work depicted on these pages. These works represent a select portion of the rich collection of the James A. Michener Art Museum, whose mission focuses largely, though not exclusively, on its surroundings.

Several factors have contributed to this lively procession. Certainly one factor is Bucks County's proximity to the major exhibition venues in New York City and Philadelphia and to the esteemed art academies in each (the National Academy of Design and the Pennsylvania Academy of the Fine Arts, respectively). This access was especially important when the county's numerous railroad stations afforded a way to travel to the cities for artists without the means to own a car. The harmonious positioning of America's foremost art schools near Bucks County ensured not only a steady stream of visiting graduates but also an influx of avant-garde influences from the cities and from artists' trips abroad, thus connecting the region to the latest movements in the field.

As William Penn had intended for the whole of Pennsylvania, Bucks County is steeped in the Quaker tradition of peaceful inclusiveness. A welcoming mind-set toward bohemian or otherwise different lifestyles has embraced newcomers through the years. And until recently, abundant affordable farmland allowed artists to be self-sufficient on an often small budget.

The sheer numbers of flourishing and exhibiting artists in the region offered camaraderie and networking opportunities as well. The highly regarded painter William Langson Lathrop (1859–1938) actively encouraged artists from the cities to stay at his home in New Hope for extended visits. His guests mingled with local artists at his legendary Sunday "teas," large gatherings that included dancing and discussions. He also led painting excursions on his boat. Ultimately, a number of his visitors settled in the area. Through these means Lathrop helped to found an important artist colony called the New Hope school (now known as the Pennsylvania impressionists). In 1929 the convivial salon atmosphere of the Lathrop home developed into the Phillips' Mill Community Association, which held annual exhibitions and is still in existence today.

Urban proximity, a culture of tolerance, and a community of artists have indeed played roles in making the county a long-running and major center for the arts. But some of these influences changed over the centuries and yet the artists have always settled in the area, and thus these factors alone cannot adequately explain the sustained fascination of the region.

Something deeper and more timeless is responsible for Bucks County's extended success as an artistic haven: the unparalleled beauty of the land itself. Its dominant and imposing natural features evoke creative responses in those attuned to the landscape and have given rise to an extraordinary canon of artistic expressions.

BUCKS COUNTY'S ARCADIAN LANDSCAPE AND THE SENSE OF PLACE

The noun "Arcadia" is defined first as an ancient Greek region frequently chosen as a background for fine arts and second as a real or imaginary place offering peace and simplicity.

The definitions are apt characterizations of Bucks County, as even a cursory drive along its length and breadth reveals. The tranquil spaces of that corner of Penn's Woods can be found amid rolling farmland studded with stone buildings, historic barns, and covered bridges. Villages and small towns clustered in the county's central and northern reaches boast active historical societies that seek to preserve their quality of life. Even the bustling larger towns in the more industrialized lower portion of the county are interspersed with protected parkland and scores of houses on the historic register.

Historic preservation is a fact of life in much of the area, a tourist mecca where bed-and-breakfast inns abound. Artists have made liberal use of the picturesque display. The Pennsylvania impressionists of the early to mid-twentieth century, for example, showed a decided sense of place in their paintings. Led by Daniel Garber (1880–1958) and Edward Redfield (1869–1965), these artists often chose their own and nearby farms or the village streets around their hometowns as subject matter for their work. Titles frequently name the exact road, valley, or farm depicted. Examples include John Folinsbee, *Bowman's Hill* (1936–37; pl. 49); George Sotter, *The Windybush Valley* (1939; pl. 56); Fern Coppedge, *Back Road to Pipersville* (n.d.; pl. 63); Edward Redfield, *Fleecydale Road* (ca. 1930; frontispiece); and Morgan Colt, *Phillips Mill Barn* (n.d.; pl. 101). In fact, the colony as a group can be said to have painted Bucks County into history.

Yet even the availability of images of rural and small-town life stops short of taking into account the glue that fastened so many artists to the area, since such scenes include mostly man-made structures. The larger explanation lies in the bones of Bucks County itself. The region is blessed with an exceptionally harmonious blend of natural formations that define an idyllic natural setting.

Hills and valleys, deeply carved rocky quarries, and ancient trees in forests shot through with streams and indigenous wildlife fill out every corner of the county. The jewels in this crown of nature are the powerful Delaware River and its adjacent canal. Running the entire length of the state, from far above the northern regions of Bucks County to Philadelphia in the south, the river is an important means of transportation for the area.

It is also a winding, watery path that presents, at nearly every bend, spectacular views that demand attention. While a wide assortment of the river's arresting prospects can be seen in works on these pages, its grandest vista, the Delaware Water Gap, is the subject of the Michener Art Museum's most famous painting, one originally created for the 1926 Sesquicentennial International Exposition held in Philadelphia. Daniel Garber based his panoramic twenty-two-foot mural, *A Wooded Watershed* (1926; pl. 36), on that celebrated gap between Pennsylvania and New Jersey. Caught between a rugged promontory in the background and a slice of forest spotted with deer in the foreground, the river is overhung with a golden mist that emphasizes this particularly dramatic bend.

Due to their preference for painting mostly *en plein air* (outdoors, directly in front of the subject depicted), many of the artists of the renowned New Hope art colony invested much of their work with a determined sense of place. Long before the twentieth-century impressionist movement, however, other styles relied just as strongly on one or another of the aspects of the Bucks County landscape.

Edward Hicks's paintings of biblical imagery (including more than sixty versions of *The Peaceable Kingdom*, illustrating the passage from Isaiah 11:6) and historic commemorations of Penn's Treaty with the Indians show his subjects against a backdrop of his native landscape. He conceives of these scenes of redemption as occurring in a place just like Bucks County. Hicks's work has fallen into American art history lore, and the regional

countryside near his home has been immortalized through his signature paintings.

Hicks is undoubtedly the most famous artist to have sprung from the county, but many nineteenth-century artists, whose styles encompass the various realist genres of the times, depended on the landscape for their work. Thomas P. Otter (1832–1890) earned his reputation by depicting local architectural landmarks as well as landscape scenes such as *The Palisades at Nockamixon* (1875; pl. 66). As impressionism arrived, followed by postimpressionism and then by the modernist movement, little changed in terms of preferred subject matter. The stunning geography continued to dominate regional artwork, though landscape forms were often reduced to shapes or outlines with large areas of pure color and unnatural lighting. While the Pennsylvania impressionists centered on the landscape more or less exactly as it was presented in nature, the modernists turned away from the sentimental quality they found in these scenes and introduced their own versions of the local views. Artists such as R.A.D. Miller, with his painting *Lace Factory* (ca. 1935; pl. 48), and Charles Ward, with *Goldie Peacock's House* (1935; pl. 62), led the march to an ever greater tendency toward pure abstraction.

The twenty-first-century art scene in Bucks County is lively. Contemporary artists explore diverse styles. Some reach back to older idioms, but presented in new ways. Others embrace abstraction or push toward conceptual art forms. Artistic expression may be far more varied today than it has been in the past, but one universal element remains constant: the influence of the landscape. Michael A. Smith, *Near Frenchtown, New Jersey* (1973; pl. 68), and Alan Goldstein, *Upriver from Lumberville Walking Bridge II* (ca. 1981; pl. 37) are two contemporary examples.

Its consummate geographic harmony, enjoyed and explored by a constant influx of creative minds, has caused Bucks County to be one of the most documented regions in the country. And since imagination and creativity are the tools of artists by definition, there is no doubt that artists will continue to interpret the landscape in new ways that secure the unbroken tradition of regional art.

WORKS ACQUIRED 1999–2002

47
EDWARD W. REDFIELD (1869–1965)
The Trout Brook ca. 1916
oil on canvas, 50 x 56 inches
James A. Michener Art Museum
Gift of Marguerite and Gerry Lenfest

Conversations with Bruce Katsiff

One of the most important gifts that the museum received in its first twenty years was the gift of fifty-nine Pennsylvania impressionist paintings from Marguerite and Gerry Lenfest. And certainly one of the most significant pictures in that collection is the dramatic *Trout Brook* by Edward Redfield. I have always enjoyed this work because it is such an evocative piece. When you stand before *Trout Brook*, you can feel the cold of the wind, you can hear the rustling of the trees, you can feel the snow landing on your head. When an artist is able to generate a response from a sense that is not just stimulated by your eyes, then that artist has produced a powerful work of art.

I became aware of Marguerite and Gerry Lenfest through newspaper stories about the possible sale of their company, Suburban Cable. I knew that they had been buying Pennsylvania impressionist pictures, and when I became aware of the pending sale, I decided to see if the Lenfests would consider the Michener as a possible place to gift their collection.

I visited the Lenfests for the first time with our then–senior curator (now Gerry and Marguerite Lenfest Chief Curator) Brian Peterson. While Brian was looking over pictures for a possible loan, Gerry and I went into his office to talk. One of his first remarks to me was: "Listen, I'm not going to give you any money." To which I responded, "Well Mr. Lenfest, I'm not here to ask for money." In return, Gerry responded, "You run a nonprofit and you *should* be here asking for money." This was my first encounter with Gerry Lenfest, and of course it developed into a terrific and important relationship, which ultimately resulted in the Lenfests' gift to the museum.

One of the most remarkable elements of the Lenfests' gift was not just their generosity with the pictures but also their recognition that the museum would need funds to properly care for the collection. When Marguerite and Gerry made their gift to the museum, they supplemented it with a $3 million unrestricted endowment to be used for hiring curatorial and registrarial staff who could care for the paintings and do the kind of research that would make the pictures all the more relevant to the community and to scholars. At the time Gerry said, "Individuals who give collections to museums should be required to give endowment money to help care for the collection."

As a result of the Lenfest gift, the museum was able to establish a curatorial position specifically overseeing the museum's collection and then to undertake the publishing of a variety of books that explored the importance of artists represented in the collection. In a very real sense, the Lenfest gift was the proof of much of what we had said about the Michener over the first years of its development. We had always argued that if the museum existed, then publicly spirited citizens in the region would consider giving their collections to this community. And that is precisely what happened with the Lenfest gift. If the Michener had not been here, those pictures would have wound up at an institution outside of Bucks County. Because the Lenfests recognized the potential of the museum and the importance of the pictures to the region, their gift catapulted the Michener into a higher orbit. After the gift the museum's exhibitions, our publications, and our standing in the region were significantly elevated.

From a recorded conversation with
Kristy Krivitsky*, November 4, 2008*

48
R.A.D. MILLER (1905–1966)
Lace Factory ca. 1935
oil on canvas, 21 x 28 inches
James A. Michener Art Museum
Gift of Marguerite and Gerry Lenfest

49
JOHN FULTON FOLINSBEE (1892–1972)
Bowman's Hill   1936–37
oil on canvas, 34 x 50 inches
James A. Michener Art Museum
Gift of Marguerite and Gerry Lenfest

50
ROBERT SPENCER (1879–1931)
A Gray Day   1912
oil on canvas, 20 x 24 inches
James A. Michener Art Museum
Gift of Marguerite and Gerry Lenfest

51
WALTER EMERSON BAUM (1884–1956)
South Side, Easton (Industrial Scene Easton) ca. 1940
oil on canvas, 28 x 37 inches
James A. Michener Art Museum
Gift of Marguerite and Gerry Lenfest

52
DANIEL GARBER (1880–1958)
Springtime in the Village   1917
oil on canvas, 30½ x 28½ inches
James A. Michener Art Museum
Gift of Marguerite and Gerry Lenfest

53
CHARLES ROSEN (1878–1950)
Opalescent Morning ca. 1909
oil on canvas, 32 x 40 inches
James A. Michener Art Museum
Gift of Marguerite and Gerry Lenfest

54
WILLIAM LANGSON LATHROP (1859–1938)
Chilmark Moor, Martha's Vineyard   1930
oil on canvas, 25 x 30 inches
James A. Michener Art Museum
Gift of Marguerite and Gerry Lenfest

55
GEORGE W. SOTTER (1879–1953)
Brace's Cove n.d.
oil on canvas, 36 x 40 inches
James A. Michener Art Museum
Gift of Marguerite and Gerry Lenfest

56
GEORGE W. SOTTER (1879–1953)
The Windybush Valley   1939
oil on board, 36 x 48 inches
James A. Michener Art Museum
Gift of Marguerite and Gerry Lenfest

BERNARD "BEN" BADURA (1896–1986)
Frame for George W. Sotter's *The Windybush Valley*   1939
carved wood with gold-leaf gilding
42¼ x 54¼ x 2¼ inches
James A. Michener Art Museum
Gift of Marguerite and Gerry Lenfest

57
KENNETH NUNAMAKER (1890–1957)
Brook in Winter 1926
oil on canvas, 44 x 50¼ inches
James A. Michener Art Museum
Gift of Marguerite and Gerry Lenfest

58
MARLENE MILLER (b. 1935)
If I Can't Have You No One Will 2001
charcoal on paper, 29¾ x 41¾ inches
James A. Michener Art Museum
Museum purchase

Conversations with Bruce Katsiff

One of the defining elements of a regional museum is the close connection between the people in a community and the institution. The audience for larger New York museums, for instance, includes many people from the city as well as tourists from around the world. The Michener, on the other hand, attracts some visitors from outside the community, but the majority of our audience comes from the Bucks County region.

With that in mind, the museum has organized projects that would closely tie the institution with the community. Our work with A Woman's Place was an excellent example of this effort. In 2002 I received a phone call from the director of A Woman's Place because she was thinking about activities that would celebrate the twenty-fifth anniversary of their organization. A Woman's Place offers services to abused women, and it maintains a facility where abused women can find housing with their children as they are making a transition out of an abusive relationship.

The museum decided to partner with them in their celebration and organize an exhibition around the theme of violence against women. Working together with A Woman's Place, the museum identified artists from the region and commissioned them to do work on this subject. One of the artists was Marlene Miller, an exceptionally skillful draftsperson whose work most often dealt with social issues, and for the exhibit she produced a series of drawings. As part of the arrangement for the project, the museum acquired work from the artists in the exhibition for the museum's collection and assisted A Woman's Place in the publication of a monograph. *A Celebration of Voices: The Twenty-fifth Anniversary of A Woman's Place* is one of several such projects that the museum has worked on with other community institutions over the past twenty years in an effort to broaden our reach and present work relevant to different audiences across the region.

From a recorded conversation with
Kristy Krivitsky, *November 4, 2008*

59
LLOYD RAYMOND NEY (1893–1965)
Study for New London Facets   1940
charcoal, graphite, and tempera on gessoed
laminated wood panel, 69¼ x 167 inches
James A. Michener Art Museum
Museum purchase and partial gift in honor of
Dr. Marvin and Muriel Sultz, Elkins Park, PA

60
LOUIS BOSA (1905–1981)
Procession 1952
oil on canvas, 40 x 62 inches
James A. Michener Art Museum
Gift of Donald E. and Anna Bosa Mulligan

61
SUSAN FENTON (b. 1949)
Profile with Lizard 1992
handpainted, toned gelatin silver print on paper, 24 x 24 inches
James A. Michener Art Museum
Museum purchase

62
CHARLES WARD (1900–1962)
Goldie Peacock's House 1935
oil on canvas, 28 x 32 inches
James A. Michener Art Museum
Museum purchase and partial gift from
Kristina Ward Turechek and Mary Ellen Ward

63
FERN I. COPPEDGE (1883–1951)
Back Road to Pipersville n.d.
oil on canvas, 38 x 40 inches
James A. Michener Art Museum
Gift of Robert J. Lillie

73
HENRY OSSAWA TANNER (1859–1937)
Christ Walking on the Water ca. 1913; print ca. 1950
etching on paper, 7¼ x 9½ inches
James A. Michener Art Museum
Gift of Samuel L. and Sheila Rosenfeld
in honor of John P. Horton

74
JEFFREY GREENE (b. 1943)
Windsail Bench   2003
ash, 52 x 86 x 46 inches
James A. Michener Art Museum
Museum purchase funded by Shirley Ellis, Carolyn Smith,
and Sandra Hardy, in Memory of Helen Bargeron Calkins

75
JOAN LINDLEY (b. 1930)
Derby 1985–86
oil on canvas, 48 x 66 inches
James A. Michener Art Museum
Museum purchase

76
JAMES LUEDERS (1927–1994)
Untitled 1973
acrylic on canvas, 76 x 96 inches
James A. Michener Art Museum
Gift of Elizabeth Osborne

77
EDWARD W. REDFIELD (1869–1965)
Early Spring   1920
oil on canvas, 38 x 50 inches
James A. Michener Art Museum
Gift of Marguerite and Gerry Lenfest
with Assistance from Wachovia

78
GEORGE W. SOTTER (1879–1953)
Untitled (Night Snow Scene) 1949
oil on canvas, 26 x 32 inches
James A. Michener Art Museum
Gift of Marguerite and Gerry Lenfest
with Assistance from Wachovia

Dancing Electrons and Dusty Skulls: Reflections on Collecting and the Power of Objects

Brian H. Peterson
Gerry and Marguerite Lenfest Chief Curator
James A. Michener Art Museum

80
ALAN MAGEE (b. 1947)
Wound 1995; printed 2004
giclée print on paper, 22 x 17 inches
James A. Michener Art Museum
Museum purchase

79
H. SCOTT HEIST (b. 1949)
Alexander Calder and White Cascades 1976
gelatin silver print on paper, 20 x 16 inches
James A. Michener Art Museum
Museum purchase

There are times when I feel like a guest on that TV game show from the sixties, *What's My Line?*—the show that required celebrities to figure out what people do for a living. The producers always managed to dig up some utterly strange occupation—"diaper service executive" or "circus sword swallower"—that was guaranteed to stump the panel. I don't know if the program ever featured an art museum curator, but had they done so even the likes of Dorothy Kilgallen and Bennett Cerf would have been left tongue-tied and dumbfounded.

If you're a scientist, a lawyer, an actor, or any number of other occupations, people have a feel for what you do every day. But curators are apparently a source of endless mystery for some folks, as indicated by the puzzled looks I get when asked about my job. Even people who work in museums have interesting ideas about the curatorial profession. Not long after I started at the Michener, one of the secretaries in our director's office asked me what a curator does. I was not prepared for this simple question, and I stammered out something stupid that I no longer remember. Her reply was, "Gee, I always thought a curator was somebody who goes around and dusts off skulls!"

Surely she's yanking my chain, I thought—but no, she was serious! To her a museum was basically a cabinet of curiosities—a place that stores wondrous and bizarre objects that do nothing but gather dust in gloomy galleries and hidden vaults. A curator is the "keeper" of all those mummies, shrunken heads, and other assorted artifacts, and these "keepers" are musty, eccentric, Dickensian characters with squinty eyes and bad posture who skulk around their precious relics muttering Latin phrases to themselves, with a ledger book in one hand and a dust cloth in the other.

This view of museums is a bit extreme. But I suspect that if you were to walk out the Michener's doors onto Pine Street or State Street, grab the first person you see, and ask him or her "What is a museum?" the response would be something like this: "A museum is a place with a big vault that stores lots of cool stuff." This description of a museum is more or less identical with the classic dictionary definition: "A depository for collecting and displaying objects having scientific, historical, or artistic value."[1]

A museum is many things: an educational institution, a gallery, a library, and a place that adds to human knowledge through research and publications. A museum also is a café, a gift shop, and a handy place to bring your visiting relatives when you can't figure out how to entertain them. But most museums are defined by the things they collect. The collection is the sine qua non, the DNA of a museum. What a museum is, what it does, how it's perceived, how it perceives itself—all grow out of the decisions about what gets stored in the vault.

Yet it's a peculiar and rather compulsive thing that we curator-types at the Michener do, when you think about it: gather together all these works of art; put them in a fireproof, bugproof, waterproof room with perfect temperature and humidity control; assign numbers to them; study them and in general treat them like the crown jewels. Which is very different from how artists treat their work, by the way. Most painters' studios are dusty, dirty, chaotic places with half-finished and barely dry pictures stacked on top of each other, and painters certainly don't wear those fancy cloth gloves when they pick up a canvas and run their greasy fingers lovingly across the surface!

So what happens between artist's studio and museum vault to transform a picture from something the artist's own mother might toss in the garbage (Van Gogh's mom was reputed to have done just that with a bunch of his canvases) into a sacred icon of art and culture? Sometimes what happens is simply that somebody decides to collect that painting, or another painting by that artist—hopefully somebody important like a big museum or maybe a Rockefeller or a Vanderbilt.

This leads to a fundamental question about the nature and purpose of museums: why are we humans so fascinated, even obsessed, with gathering together these sacred objects?

It's not just museums that do this—there are those aforementioned scions of commerce, as well as our namesake James A. Michener, whose art collection began at age seven with magazine reproductions of paintings pasted onto pieces of cardboard and blossomed into world-class accumulations of paintings and prints. Michener recorded his rather humorous thoughts on the subject in an essay on his famous collection of American art, some pieces of which we're lucky enough to have on our own walls:

The typical collector is a male, usually unbalanced in some direction, who, if he were normal, would not need to collect odd bits and pieces. I believe that any collector of anything suffers from some kind of mental or psychological aberration, and that his collecting is a therapy which may run into a great deal of expense but which protects his sanity and allows him to operate in other fields fairly normally. I believe that this generalized description would fit the vast majority of collectors. I know it fits me. If I were a completely well-balanced person, I would not need to collect.[2]

I can't help but wonder what a bland and featureless world we would inhabit if everyone were "completely well-balanced." I'll take a reasonable amount of mental aberration over well-balanced any day of the week, because it's the quirks, tics, and oddities of our personalities that lead us into interesting and creative lives, as well as interesting and creative collections. As Tolstoy said in the famous opening line of *Anna Karenina*: "Happy families are all alike. Every unhappy family is unhappy in its own way."

Michener's self-deprecating humor aside, the question remains, why do we do it? Why do individuals and institutions compete with each other so fiercely to create the finest collection of Chinese export cups, pewter spoons, glass insulators, yard ornaments, model trains—or Pennsylvania impressionist paintings? Are we really so aberrant and unbalanced, or could there be other reasons why we engage in this apparently bizarre practice?

❧

I'm thinking of medieval pilgrims who were known to walk for hundreds of miles simply to be in the presence of what they believed to be one of the baby teeth of Jesus, or a piece of the True Cross, or the dried remains of a drop or two of the Virgin's milk.

I'm thinking of a story told by a fellow curator about the intense excitement he felt as a kid when he was allowed to take a swing with one of Babe Ruth's actual bats, and how this experience was what led him to want to work in a museum.

I'm thinking about a more recent TV show called *The Dead Zone*, based on a Stephen King story in which a guy gets eerie visions and cryptic information simply from touching a doorknob, a desk lamp, or some other random object that had been touched previously by a perfect stranger.

We like to see ourselves as rational creatures who make decisions based on a dispassionate, logical assessment of right and wrong, good and bad, healthy and unhealthy. But our ideas and fantasies about objects reveal that the veneer of civilization is indeed thin. The logical, civilized parts of our brain don't really believe that some mysterious personal essence is left on an object after someone touches it, or that the object actually becomes a conduit to another person's consciousness, or that an object is a magical vessel that stores up some weird psychic energy like a double-A battery of the soul! But clearly there's an elemental, uncivilized part of our mind that's activated in the presence of certain kinds of objects, and this has a lot to do with why we collect them.

The idea that there is a mysterious power in objects runs very deep in the human psyche. In Polynesian and Melanesian cultures, for example, great importance is placed on something called *mana*, a supernatural, sacred force that resides in people, animals, and things. One can be born with mana, but one can also acquire it, through warfare or, interestingly enough, by owning objects that are thought to possess it. So if a prosperous person has an amulet that contains mana, and that person gives the amulet to a friend, then the former's power and good fortune will likely be transferred to the latter.

Could it be that something similar is going on when, in Michener's words, we "collect odd bits and pieces?" Could Michener's "psychological aberration" actually be an expression of an ancient and primal experience of connection with the things around us that lurks in the depths of our enlightened modern minds? Why else would we be so maniacally focused on the *authenticity* of an object? We need to know that it's the "real thing," meaning, its ancestry can be traced through provenance, science, and connoisseurship back to the original owner or maker, whose essence or mana is somehow transferred through the decades and centuries all the way to me, the fella who shelled out some dough at an auction or on eBay. As the owner of the authentic object, I acquire the power that comes from its magical connection to the legendary heroes and events that created it or used it or in some way blessed it with their spirit and essence. My mana is increased.

I suppose this is evidence of mental aberration, as Michener suggests, especially if the need to collect becomes compulsive. Perhaps if one felt completely confident and emotionally grounded, one would not need to constantly bathe one's soul in the power (real or imagined) of magical objects. But it would be a mistake to overpsychologize the need to collect—to reduce it to some minor insecurity that could easily be healed with the right combination of positive thinking and psychotropic drugs. The reason this would be a mistake is that *objects are powerful.*

I'm thinking of Bill Gates—not because my computer is malfunctioning, but because of something I once read about his famous house in Medina, Washington. Apparently the walls are dotted with giant computer screens, and Mr. Bill and his guests can access the entire visual heritage of the world with the click of a mouse.

Can't make it to the Louvre to see the Mona Lisa? No problem—just find the image in your handy computer database and there she is, smile and all.

Gates doesn't think objects are powerful. In his universe, paintings are simply another form of information that can be easily digitized and disseminated. But given a choice between the actual Mona and an image on a monitor, which one would *you* pick? I suspect Mona on canvas would win out, in part because a trip to Paris would be necessary, but mainly because there really is a difference between the entity itself and a bunch of illuminated pixels on a screen. I could go into a lengthy discourse on the effect of the surface of the painting, on its size, on its subtlety of color and line, on a hundred other qualities both tangible and intangible that both computer monitor and coffee-table books can't reproduce. But I don't want to insult your intelligence.

It's not that reproductions aren't useful—but haul one of those books into a museum gallery sometime and compare the reproductions to the originals. Take it from me, the experience can be scary—especially if you wrote the book!

Even a hardened skeptic might concede that a painting is a powerful object, because a painting has intrinsic qualities such as surface and color that give it character and presence. But can the same be said for Babe Ruth's bat? Suppose someone hands me an old baseball bat and I take a swing. Whatever. Then I'm told that the bat belonged to Babe Ruth, and all the stories I heard about the great man when I was a kid rush into my mind. Suddenly beams of light flow out from the nondescript piece of wood in my hands, and it's no longer just a bat, it's special, it's magic, it's a direct connection to the mythic days of yore. Now when I take a swing I can almost see "the Babe" pointing to the stands and hear the crowd in Yankee Stadium roar as the ball disappears over the fence.

What percentage of this experience flows from my vivid imagination versus some intrinsic power that flows from the object itself? The most intelligent, rational answer to this question is that imagination is everything. It is patently ridiculous to think otherwise. And yet we do. Call it unscientific, call it primitive—but there's a bit of the mana-worshiping Polynesian tribesperson in all of us. We live in a culture that places intense value on objects, value that far exceeds any rational justifications we might conjure up to preserve our dignity as logical beings.

If you need evidence, look no further than the American Association of Museums, which says that in our country alone there are approximately 20,000 museums, most of which are repositories for iconic objects of various kinds. You could also look at all the auction houses, galleries, dealers, and websites whose existence depends on the idea that people will pay lots of money for things they may have never seen, but which are deemed important for one reason or another by folks like me, the "experts" (a.k.a. shamans or high priests of mana-land) who have been given the power to increase or decrease the mana quotient of objects.

We may look down on those "ignorant" medieval peasants who sacrificed large portions of their lives just to stand a few feet away from a single thorn from the True Crown of Thorns. But we're really not that different. Instead of making a pilgrimage to Constantinople to see the head of John the Baptist (people actually used to do that), we pack our kids in the car and travel to the museum to see the mummified remains of King Tut or a landscape by Cézanne or, if you live in Bucks County, by Edward Redfield and Daniel Garber.

When you stand in front of that Garber landscape, you're free to admire its transcendental beauty as well as study the brilliance of its visual rhythms and subtle colors. But if you were to be totally honest, you'd have to admit that much of your enjoyment comes from the subterranean pleasure of immersing yourself in the strange magic of the object itself, which was touched by the steady hand of the artist and somehow connects you directly both to him and the world he inhabited.

"Gee," you might say to yourself, "not only is this a beautiful picture, but the guy made it just up the road from here!" In fact you could probably still find the spot where Garber planted his easel, and the view might not have changed that much. This is a common pastime among Bucks County collectors, by the way, and it's more evidence of what we'll call the "mana factor." Not only do you own the painting, you know where it was made, and have stood in the very place where the great man stood. Some of Garber's mana has flowed down the mana pipeline, your mana cup runneth over, and as the Psalm says, surely goodness and mercy shall follow you all the days of your life.

The fact that Garber lived and worked just up the road is meaningful because it personalizes the picture—makes it downright neighborly, something you can connect with and "own" even if you can't afford to buy it. But there's another layer to the experience of a Garber landscape that's less personal and more collective. Garber has captured not only his own private vision of a Bucks County quarry or village, he's encapsulated or distilled something of the essence of Bucks County itself—not only its topographical features, but its particular nature as a particular region with a particular history.

It's as though the artist's easel sprouts roots that burrow into the very soul of the place, and the image that emerges from those roots both expresses that soul and helps bring it to life. When a bunch of artists do this, as happened in Bucks County in the early twentieth century, people begin to recognize the "feel" of their corner of the universe in the work, not only as individuals but as a community. A sense of ownership, even pride, is born. These pictures are *our* pictures. This is who we are.

In other words, Bucks County without the Michener Art Museum is like a home without the paintings and family photographs on the walls. It would still be a home, but a home without a history—without a heart. This is why the Michener and most other museums use a lot of high-toned phrases when describing our collections: cultural patrimony, regional heritage, public trust, etc. In a very real sense we don't own what's on our walls and in our vault. You do.

This is also why museums have strict rules about how we dispose of or "deaccession" objects, and about how we care for the things in our vault— because these objects are only technically owned by us. The assumption is that they are really owned by the community. We hold them in trust for the community, and it's our job to make sure that they're still here a hundred years from now—maybe five hundred years—or whatever "in perpetuity" means. If we mismanage our collection, we abuse that trust and there will be serious moral (and legal) repercussions.

All this "soul" and "community ownership" and "public trust" stuff may seem like an impossible burden for a layer of multicolored paint on a piece of canvas. How can we expect a painting to reflect the unique character of both its maker and the place where it was made, so it becomes a kind of container or vessel of cultural information that's passed down through the generations? Yet this is a common feature

of art that people care about, art that lasts. Think of all the great writers who lived and breathed the unique persona of a country or region: William Faulkner and Mississippi. Herman Melville and Massachusetts. It's not just American writers who do this, of course. Russians learn what it means to be Russian from Pushkin and Dostoevsky. The English have Shakespeare, the Spanish have Cervantes, the Irish have Yeats. Would anyone deny that there's something uniquely French about Monet, or uniquely German about Bach, or uniquely American about Winslow Homer, or uniquely Philadelphian about Thomas Eakins?

The Bucks County pantheon doesn't necessarily include folks of the caliber of Shakespeare and Bach! Yet in their own humble way, our region's artists have done the same thing for Bucks County that William Wordsworth did for rural England and Nathaniel Hawthorne did for rural New England: make works of art that grow out of the soil of a place, that people immediately recognize as theirs.

But really—come on—isn't this a lot of sentimental hooey? Is it possible, truly possible, for a geographical entity to have an identity, a soul? Is it possible that generation after generation of people living and dying in a place can build up legends, recollections, and experiences that slowly coalesce and congeal, weaving themselves together into a story? Is it possible that artists hear this story in the rhythms of language and see it in the morning light falling on a farmhouse surrounded by a field of new snow? Is it possible that these artists not only tell this collective story, but add to it, become part of it, until a quarry is not just a quarry, it's the quarry that Daniel Garber painted, and a bridge is not just a bridge, it's the bridge that was built when the old one burned down—you know, the one that Redfield painted right after the lightning strike in 1923?

The answer is yes, it's possible, in fact it happens in many places, including Bucks County, Pennsylvania. The Michener Art Museum exists to tell that story, and the way we tell it is through books and exhibits and classes and lectures. But mainly we tell the story through the things that we care for and are entrusted with—not dusty skulls, but paintings, sculptures, photographs, prints, most of which were made in Bucks County or by Bucks County artists.

FIREPLACE BY PHILLIP LLOYD POWELL, ACQUIRED 2008

Conversations with Bruce Katsiff

Artists enrich us not only with their work but also with their dynamic personalities. One such individual was Phil Powell. Phil passed away in 2008, and after his death I began to think about how much he would be missed and wrote this reminiscence:

Dancer, traveler, biker, woodworker, and a regular member of the breakfast club at Sneddon's, Phil helped to teach us all how to better love life without the burdens of money, power, and social position. His vast network of friends and admirers spanned several continents and radiated out from its nexus in the little town of New Hope. With the flash of one earring and the glow of his smile, Phil made every encounter an exploration of life's pleasures. He found joy in every conversation and value in every culture. In India, in Europe, in New York, and in Lambertville, Phil explored his world with an open heart and an engaging personality that motivated many of us to shout, "Life is good and Phil knows it."

At sixty, at seventy, and even at eighty, Phil seemed to increase in energy and joy. On a bike few could match his stamina as he almost effortlessly peddled up the hill to Rosemont. He taught us all that age was indeed a state of mind, and in Phil's mind he was ageless. Few of us who knew him will ever forget his spirit or abandon our own desire to find some small piece of the joy in life that Phil seemed to gulp with every breath.

Phil Powell was a bright light in our universe, and he still shines in our hearts and memories.

Shortly after Phil's death, the museum learned about a pending sale at Rago Arts and Auction Center in Lambertville of objects made by Phil and his partner, Paul Evans. Of particular interest to us was a fireplace mantel Phil made ca. 1956–58 that had been exhibited in the shop that he and Paul ran in New Hope. We went to the auction with a limit on what the museum could spend, and when the hammer fell we were fortunately the high bidder. Afterward I mused that Phil might visit me in a dream and say, "Bruce, you didn't buy that piece when I was alive, but you bought it after I was dead!" But, truly, I had no guilt about this, because the museum had commissioned Phil to do several pieces while he was alive, including a bench and a whimsical groundbreaking shovel.

Woodworking has a strong tradition within Bucks County. We were honored to see Phil's fireplace join our collection of work by distinguished woodworkers like George Nakashima, Robert Whitley, Mark Sfirri, and Jeffrey Greene.

From a recorded conversation with
Kristy Krivitsky, *February 19, 2009*

81
PHILLIP LLOYD POWELL (1919–2008)
Fireplace ca.1956–58
walnut, 97½ x 67 x 6 inches
James A. Michener Art Museum
Museum purchase funded by the Janus Society,
Beveridge Moore and Henry Morof Trust, and
George C. Benson in honor of his friend John Horton

82

JONATHAN K. TREGO (1817–1901)

Smith Trego   ca. 1840

oil on fabric, 25⅛ x 21¼ inches

James A. Michener Art Museum

Museum purchase funded by Margaret M. Ahlum,

Mrs. Lewis Hall, and Henry Morof

83
JONATHAN K. TREGO (1817–1901)
Anna Phillips Trego   ca. 1840
oil on fabric, 25⅛ x 21⅜ inches
James A. Michener Art Museum
Museum purchase funded by Margaret M. Ahlum,
Mrs. Lewis Hall, and Henry Morof

84
RICARDO BARROS (b. 1953)
Isaac Witkin 1996
carbon pigment digital print on paper, 25⅜ x 24 inches
James A. Michener Art Museum
Museum purchase funded by the Bette and
G. Nelson Pfundt Photography Endowment

85
EMMET GOWIN (b. 1941)
Nancy, Danville 1969
toned gelatin silver print on paper, 5½ x 7 inches
James A. Michener Art Museum
Gift of Emmet and Edith Gowin

86
EDMUND BRUCE ECKSTEIN (b. 1943)
May Day Rally (Philadelphia, May 1969) 1969
printed April 2007
gelatin silver print on paper, 16 x 20 inches
James A. Michener Art Museum
Museum purchase funded by the Bette and
G. Nelson Pfundt Photography Endowment

87
EDMUND BRUCE ECKSTEIN (b. 1943)
Basic Training, Fort Jackson South Carolina 1970
printed April 2007
gelatin silver print on paper, 16 x 20 inches
James A. Michener Art Museum
Museum purchase funded by the Bette and
G. Nelson Pfundt Photography Endowment

88
MICHAEL BECOTTE (b. 1945)
Construction #339   2003
iris print on paper, 28 x 36 inches
James A. Michener Art Museum
Museum purchase funded by the Bette and
G. Nelson Pfundt Photography Endowment

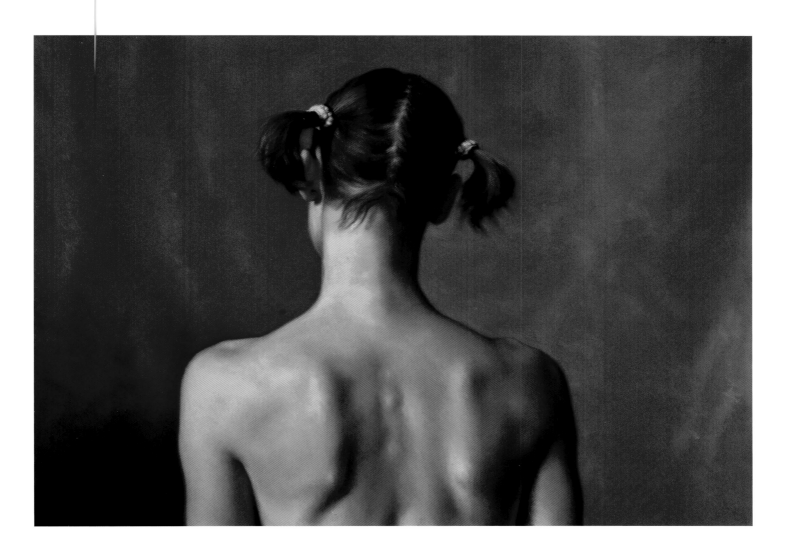

89
NELSON SHANKS (b. 1937)
Pigtails   2004
oil on canvas, 19½ x 27¾
James A. Michener Art Museum
Museum purchase funded by the Janus Society
© 2004 Nelson Shanks

90
ROBERT GWATHMEY (1903–1988)
End of Day 1943
oil on canvas, 30 x 36 inches
James A. Michener Art Museum
Gift of the John P. Horton Estate
Art © Estate of Robert Gwathmey /
Licensed by VAGA, New York, NY

91
ISAAC WITKIN (1936–2006)
Waif's Anchors 1986
patinated bronze, 119 x 102 x 36 inches
James A. Michener Art Museum
Gift in memory of Robert V. Nesi by his family

92
WILLIAM A. SMITH (1918–1989)
Portrait of George Nakashima   1988–89
oil on canvas, 43¾ x 41¼ inches
James A. Michener Art Museum
Gift of Kevin Nakashima and Mira Nakashima-Yarnall

93
ALAN MAGEE (b. 1947)
Countermeasure 2004
acrylic on canvas, 50 x 75 inches
James A. Michener Art Museum
Museum purchase funded by the Janus Society
© Alan Magee, 2004

96
MAVIS SMITH (b. 1956)
Sink or Swim   2004
egg tempera on gesso panel, 26 x 28 inches
James A. Michener Art Museum
Museum purchase funded by Lorraine Nevens Greenberg

97
GUY PÈNE DU BOIS (1884–1958)
In the Courtroom n.d.
oil on canvas, 17 x 24 inches
James A. Michener Art Museum
Gift of the John P. Horton Estate

98
BEN SHAHN (1898–1969)
Study for Riker's Island Mural ca. 1934
tempera on paper, 11 x 33 inches
James A. Michener Art Museum
Gift of George Benson in Honor of John Horton
Art © Estate of Ben Shahn / Licensed by VAGA, New York, NY

99
EMILY BROWN (b. 1943)
Fond Farewell 2002
ink on paper, 52 x 96 inches
James A. Michener Art Museum
Museum purchase funded by D. Kenneth Leiby

Les lichens   The lichens   SL

101
MORGAN COLT (1876–1926)
Phillips Mill Barn n.d.
oil on canvas, 19½ x 23½ inches
James A. Michener Art Museum
Gift of Marguerite and Gerry Lenfest

100
ED COLKER (b. 1927)
The Summons of Becoming: Poems by René Char 2007
translated by Mary Ann Caws with hand-colored
lithographs as pochoir by Ed Colker
published by Haybarn Press, 2007
cloth portfolio book, printed letterpress
by Bradley Hutchinson; limited edition
9 x 14 inches
James A. Michener Art Museum
Museum purchase

104
ARTHUR MELTZER (1893–1989)
Summer Skies 1924
oil on canvas, 22¼ x 32⅛ inches
James A. Michener Art Museum
Gift of Remak Ramsay

105
RAE SLOAN BREDIN (1880–1933)
After the Rain   1913
oil on canvas, 30 x 40
James A. Michener Art Museum
Museum purchase funded by the Janus Society,
the Beveridge Moore and Henry Morof Trust,
and John C. Seegers

106
EUGENE HIGGINS (1874–1958)
A Connecticut Ploughman n.d.
oil on canvas, 26 x 33 inches
James A. Michener Art Museum
Gift of the John P. Horton Estate

107
WILLIAM SCHWARTZ (1896–1977)
Come to Me All Ye That Are Heavy Laden   1934
oil on canvas, 40 x 50
James A. Michener Art Museum
Gift of the John P. Horton Estate

108
CHARLES ROSEN (1878–1950)
Quarry and Crusher ca. early 1930s
oil on canvas, 32 x 40 inches
James A. Michener Art Museum
Museum purchase funded by George C. Benson
in honor of his friend John Horton

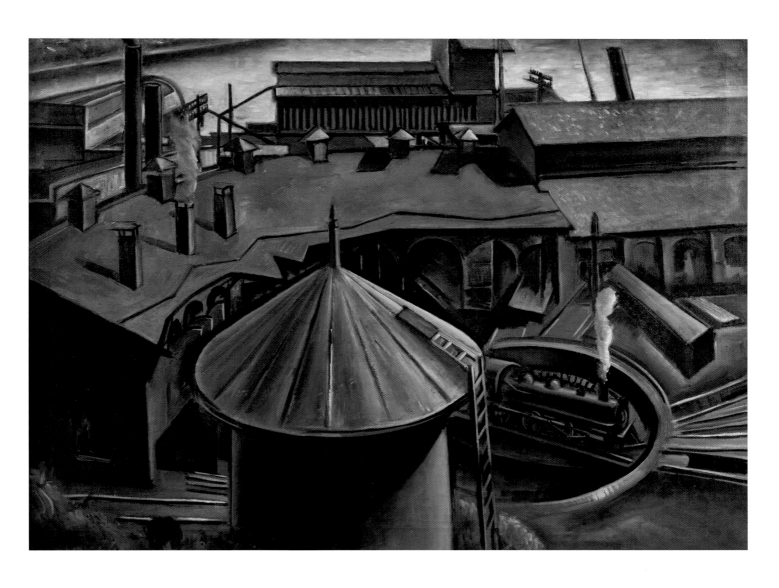

109
CHARLES ROSEN (1878–1950)
The Roundhouse, Kingston, New York   1927
oil on canvas, 30⅛ x 40¼ inches
James A. Michener Art Museum
Gift of the John P. Horton Estate

110
WILLIAM LANGSON LATHROP (1859–1938)
Lathrop Sketchbook #9   1898–1904
pencil on paper, 8½ x 5¼ inches
James A. Michener Art Museum
Gift of Tom Buckley

wall light gray
with a trace of yellow.

Roof red & gray.
wall pink buff.   July 14.
'04

New Hope, June 23

111
RANDALL EXON (b. 1956)
Beach House 2002
oil on canvas, 36 x 36 inches
James A. Michener Art Museum
Museum purchase funded by the Janus Society

112
STEPHEN GUION WILLIAMS (b. 1942)
Sunrise, Chosen Land 1972
gelatin silver print on paper, 20¾ x 13⅞ inches
James A. Michener Art Museum
Museum purchase funded by the Bette and
G. Nelson Pfundt Photography Endowment

113
FREDERICK WILLIAM HARER (1879–1948)
Desk and Sidechair ca. 1930s
walnut with pear and ebony inlay and upholstered slip seat
34½ x 38 x 22½ inches (desk), 30 x 17¾ x 17 inches (chair)
James A. Michener Art Museum
Museum purchase funded by John C. Seegers

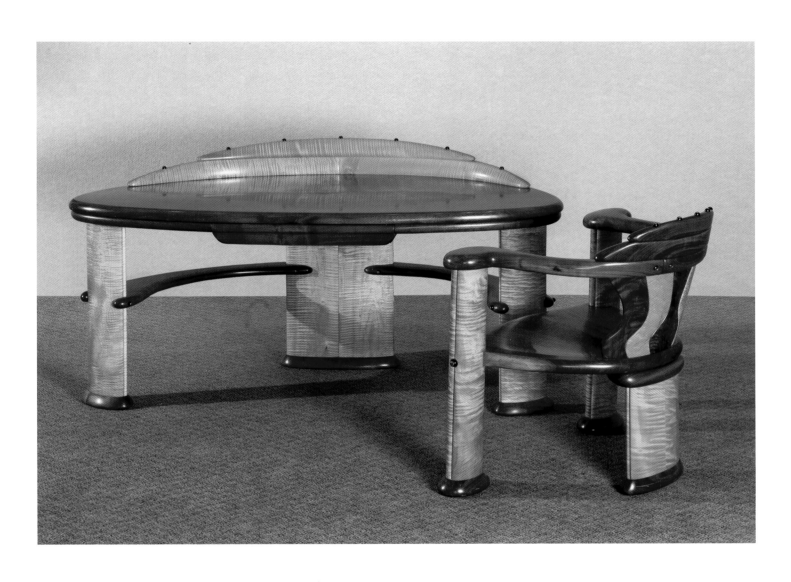

114
ROBERT WHITLEY (b. 1924)
Throne Desk and Armchair 1999
curly maple, American black walnut, bird's-eye maple, and
dogwood with ebony pegs
33½ x 64 x 32 inches (desk), 34 x 34¼ x 27 inches (armchair)
James A. Michener Art Museum
Gift of Steve and Suzanne Kalafer and
Flemington Car and Truck Country Family of Dealerships

115
CATHERINE JANSEN (b. 1950)
The Blue Room   1970
photosensitized cloth, photographic dyes
James A. Michener Art Museum
Museum purchase and partial gift from artist

BUILDING NEW WORLDS: A HUNDRED YEARS OF ART IN BUCKS COUNTY AND BEYOND

Brian H. Peterson

We know we belong to the land, and the land we belong to is grand!
—Oscar Hammerstein II, 1943, from *Oklahoma!*

We belong to the land. Hammerstein's lyric is one of the most familiar phrases in the history of American musicals. When you hear that sentence sung on stage, it's accompanied by a legion of high-kicking, arm-waving erstwhile Oklahomans who are just about the happiest people on earth.

But what the heck was the venerable Oscar talking about?

We belong to the land. "Belong" implies ownership. But the land doesn't own us. We own the land. It says so on the deed to my house, which tells me how much territory I possess, the shape of the lot, and the exact latitude and longitude of each corner. Land is something we buy, sell, claim, trade for, fight over, dig into, and live on. There's never any question about who owns whom.

But Hammerstein's swirling legions are singing a different tune. *We belong to the land.* In other words, the land was here before we arrived and will be here after we're gone. The land is big, like the universe is big, so big that we can be part of it—no, we *are* it. The connection is so profound that the two entities—land and us—are joined, each with roots sunk deep into the other. The land's atoms and our atoms are somehow the same atoms.

Hammerstein probably wrote that line while standing at his writing desk in his Doylestown home, which is only a mile or two away from where I'm sitting in my museum office. He was writing about an imaginary Oklahoma, of course, an Oklahoma of the mind. Still, it's interesting that he was staring out his office window at the gentle, tree-covered hills of Bucks County rather than the Oklahoma plains when he penned those fifteen immortal words. There's just something about Bucks County—the place itself, not the lines on a map—something that has stirred the imaginations of creative people for a long, long time.

Hammerstein's lyric could have been written forty years earlier by one of Bucks County's famous landscape painters—that is, if there had been a painter who could write in anapestic trimeter, who had the courage to repeat the word "we" three times in the same sentence along with "land" twice and "we belong to" twice, who understood the power of simplicity and concocted a line whose fifteen words have only seventeen syllables.

By 1903 these landscape painters had begun to arrive here—first Lathrop and Redfield, then Rosen, Spencer, and Garber. The floodgates opened and dozens poured in, hundreds even, until every square inch of Bucks County's land ended up depicted in somebody's picture, and the terms "New Hope school" and "Pennsylvania impressionism" worked their way into the standard lingo of American art.

Why did those legions of brush-waving, canvas-toting bohemians come here to ply their trade? Did they want to belong to the land, like Oscar's Oklahomans?

Many American painters had cut their teeth in Europe. Many had studied in France. Many had even lived at Giverny, the famous home of the master Claude Monet—the same Monet who said, "All my money goes into my garden." These painters came back to America filled with visions of French farmland and French meadows and French gardens. They had enjoyed the camaraderie of like minds at places like Giverny, and they were possessed by a desire to re-create these conditions on American soil. They wanted to find some *land* to live on and paint, land they could be part of—as long as it also had electricity, running water, and decent train service to a metropolitan area where they could display their wares.

What happened in Bucks County in the early twentieth century was one current in a much larger stream, a stream that flowed over most of the civilized world. Artists wanted to make pictures that said to a forest or a hill, I'm over here and you're over there—let's talk to each other. But these artists were not Thoreau wannabes who lived alone in their cabins and huts, searching for a pure life of contemplation and solitude. No, these painters sought out *each other* almost as much as they sought out the valleys, rivers, and picturesque villages that populated their canvases.

It was as though they had heard the voice of some Biblical prophet who commanded them to be fruitful with their brushes, multiply their canvases, and spread out across the landscape—to Branchville and Provincetown, New Hope and Old Lyme, Taos and Cos Cob. To Indiana, California, South Carolina, and Minnesota, not to mention a plethora of places outside our borders, from Toronto to Stockholm to Istanbul.

These artists loved the territory they painted. They were less inspired by the Book of Genesis, which says we "have dominion over the fish of the sea and the birds of the air," and more inspired by the gentle words of the Psalmist who said, "Faithfulness springs forth from the earth. . . . and our land will yield its harvest."

One can speculate about why this need to connect with the land was part of the artistic zeitgeist of the early twentieth century. It might have been nostalgia for simpler times—a reaction to the mechanistic excesses of the industrial revolution. It might have been a genuine need to hook up with the inner life of the natural world, as Wordsworth did, along with Emerson, Thoreau, Constable, and countless lesser-known artists and intellectuals in the eighteenth and nineteenth centuries. Or it might have been an instinctive need to anchor themselves firmly to the ground, to avoid being swamped by an impending tidal wave: a tidal wave of ideas. If the late nineteenth and early twentieth centuries were, at least in part, the era of "we belong to the land," then the rest of the twentieth century was the era of ideas.

Think of the ideas that sweep across the cultural landscape in the twentieth century, starting with Picasso and Braque and Kandinsky: the idea that art is no longer married to what the eye sees. The *elements* of seeing—line, shape, rhythm, movement—are more important in a painting than what is actually seen.

Ideas. An object is depicted from all sides on a two-dimensional surface. An object is broken into subsets and components, disassembled and reassembled into a barely recognizable conglomeration. Objects disappear entirely, and color, gesture, and movement take over, first tied to the rhythms of the body, then removed from the body and turned into pure abstraction. Eventually the lines, shapes, and gestures are reduced to almost nothing, and a painting becomes a simple color, or a thin stripe across a monochromatic canvas, or a few seemingly random strokes in an empty field.

Many people still were insisting that a painting must look like what we see. But along come Dalí and Magritte, who contend that a melting clock or a train speeding into a chimney are just as real, perhaps even more real, because the *mind* is the ultimate reality.

Even in the earlier landscape era, when art colonies are springing up like dandelions, plenty of folks still believe that a painting must be about a grand Biblical story, a victorious general, or a Greek god. But then Marcel Duchamp declares that a urinal is just as interesting. By paying attention to that urinal he forces people to see it differently, to appreciate the beauty of the commonplace. And he helps give birth to the idea that art is about ideas.

Some artists—descendants of Duchamp—become commentators and rebels, acutely aware of the dangers of cultural norms and oppressive patriarchies. These artists are gentle warriors who are committed to changing the world with their art. They dedicate their lives, as they might word it, to battling the rigid hermeneutics of hegemonic authoritarian dictatorial power structures. Their passion is genuine, but perhaps they could use some help from Hammerstein in the language arena, especially his love of one-syllable words!

Ideas and more ideas in the onrushing tsunami of ideas, ideas that often become movements and genres: academy realism begets the Ashcan school begets regionalism begets the figurative revival begets photo realism. Expressionism begets abstract expressionism begets minimalism begets pop art begets op art begets postmodernism begets neoromanticism. All this begetting, idea after idea, each one trumping the last, until finally artists grow weary of the begetting game and ask themselves, Which of these ideas, this history, these styles and techniques and media and "isms"—which ones matter to *me*, which ones can't I live without?

So it turns out that Bucks County in the twentieth century was a microcosm of what happened in the big wide world. In the beginning was the art colony: a more or less cohesive group of artists all living and working in the same place, painting the land each in their own way, but sharing similar values and similar subjects.

By the end of the twentieth century the art colony was a distant memory, but there were even more artists, probably ten times as many artists per square mile. These artists were practicing countless different styles, using endless different techniques, and had mastered a dizzying array of different mediums. There were painters, photographers, sculptors, woodworkers, printmakers, craft artists, video artists, conceptual artists. There were the self-taught and the highly trained, the avant-garde and the derriere-garde, the poetic dreamers and the hard-nosed observers.

And now, in 2009, if you go to one of the annual juried shows in Bucks County, you will see traditional landscapes, still lifes, and portraits; pure abstraction, not-so-pure abstraction, and intense realism; dreamlike tableaux, political commentary, and even a few grand storytellers in the tradition of Rubens and Poussin. Anything and everything is available to the artist of today. Instead of being intimidated by all these possibilities, artists are intrepid explorers and fearless assimilators, eagerly grabbing whatever they need so they can build the worlds they need to build.

If the art of the early twentieth century was militantly regional and parochial (while still

1985 The old facility that housed the Bucks County prison closes and the warden's house is placed on the National Register of Historic Buildings and Sites.

1987 The historic facility is chosen as the site for the James A. Michener Arts Center, named in honor of one of Bucks County's most prominent citizens, the world-renowned writer and Pulitzer Prize–winner James A. Michener, who grew up in Doylestown, Pennsylvania.

1988 In September six thousand visitors attend the art center's opening, which includes a parade with Jim Michener. Herman Silverman is named president of the board of trustees.

1990 Bruce Katsiff is appointed director/CEO. Under his direction the board of trustees approves the name change to the James A. Michener Art Museum to align more closely with the mission to operate as a museum with a focus on collecting work from the Bucks County region.

1992 The Michener Art Endowment Challenge is initiated by the famous author. This program challenges the museum to secure at least forty museum-quality works over a one-year period. Michener himself pledges $500,000 to create an endowment to care for the donated artwork. In all, fifty-five donors contributed 189 works, including paintings, works on paper, and sculpture representing forty-two Bucks County–area artists.

Dr. D. Kenneth Leiby donates fourteen paintings to the museum, including works by Bucks County artists Daniel Garber, William Lathrop, George Sotter, Henry Snell, M. Elizabeth Price, and others.

On June 10 a groundbreaking ceremony attended by James and Mari Michener marks the start of a new $1.65 million expansion of museum facilities.

1993 The museum reopens following the expansion project, which more than doubles the institution's size. The major features include the addition of the Grand Entrance Hall, four new galleries, an outdoor sculpture garden, a family education center, art storage vaults, and a museum shop and café.

1994 Woodworkers from the Mid-Atlantic region are invited to enter a competition to create a one-of-a

kind bench. The winning proposal is submitted by master craftsman and furniture designer Robert Whitley, whose bench is ultimately placed in the Grand Entrance Hall.

A $1.5 million gift for a new wing and expansion is bequeathed to the museum by Mari Sabusawa, James Michener's late wife. This helps to fulfill the couple's longtime dream to honor artists of all disciplines.

The museum acquires Daniel Garber's *A Wooded Watershed*. This mural had been installed in the stage backdrop at the Mont Alto campus of Pennsylvania State University and then forgotten for sixty years. The university agrees to send the painting to the Michener Art Museum in return for a scholarship endowment in Garber's name.

1995 The groundbreaking for the new Mari Sabusawa Michener Wing begins.

Carolyn Calkins Smith is named president of the board of trustees.

1996 The Garber mural is installed as the keystone of the museum's permanent collection.

A $5.5 million gift from James Michener and his late wife, Mari, is pledged to the Doylestown Cultural District. The gift represents one of the largest ever given to the community. Michener contributes $3.5 million to the endowment of the James A. Michener Art Museum; the Bucks County Free Library and Mercer Museum each receive $1 million.

On October 27 the Mari Sabusawa Michener Wing opens. The wing features *Creative Bucks County: A Celebration of Art and Artists,* a long-term installation that includes a video theater, interactive computer database stations, and individual exhibits on twelve well-known Bucks County artists who worked in the visual, performing, and literary arts.

1997 In March the only three existing portraits of Edward Hicks—the nineteenth-century primitive painter— are brought to the James A. Michener Art Museum for a special exhibit. Each painting was done by Thomas Hicks, Edward's younger cousin. Two of these paintings were created while Edward was alive, and the third was created after his death. The third portrait of Hicks is discovered in a New York art gallery by two decorative arts and antique dealers from Bucks County, who contact the director of the museum, and the painting is subsequently acquired for the permanent collection largely through funds from the community and from members of the Newtown Friends Meeting.

1999 H. F. "Gerry" Lenfest and his wife, Marguerite, make the largest donation of artwork to the museum in its history—fifty-nine paintings of Pennsylvania impressionism, supplemented with a $3 million endowment to help care for the works. Upon receipt, the museum has become the primary repository for art made in Bucks County. The gift includes works by Edward Redfield, Daniel Garber, Fern Coppedge, Robert Spencer, and other celebrated artists who worked in the area.

2000 The Putman Smith Gallery is renovated to house the newly donated paintings that will be exhibited in a long-term installation titled *The Lenfest Exhibition of Pennsylvania Impressionism.*

In September the Patricia D. Pfundt Sculpture Garden opens to the public. The sculpture garden, made possible through the generosity of the Pfundt family, is a long-awaited goal of the museum and houses a growing collection of American sculpture.

2001 The Michener Art Museum receives accreditation by the American Association of Museums. Accreditation certifies that a museum operates according to national standards set forth by the museum profession, manages its collections responsibly, and provides quality service to the public. Of the eight thousand museums nationwide that are members of the American Association of Museums, only some 750 are accredited.

2003 Edward G. Biester Jr. is named president of the board of trustees.

In September the museum opens a new gallery space. The Commonwealth of Pennsylvania Gallery is made possible through support from former Governor Mark Schweiker, Governor Ed Rendell, former State Senator Joseph Conti, and State Representative Charles T. McIlhinney Jr. and features works by twentieth-century American artists from the museum's permanent collection.

In November, thanks to the generous gift of a twenty-year rent-free lease by developer George E. Michael, along with a significant fundraising effort from public and private donors, the museum opens a five-thousand-square-foot satellite facility in the Union Square complex in New Hope. The New

Hope location extends and continues the Michener Art Museum's tradition of collecting, preserving, and interpreting the art of the Bucks County region.

2004 The museum celebrates the addition of the new G. Nelson Pfundt Gallery, which is made possible by a gift from the Pfundt family trust.

2006 William Denison Williams, a member of the James A. Michener Art Museum, bequeaths an unrestricted gift of more than $6 million to the museum, representing the largest cash gift in the museum's history. Williams and his wife, Virginia, were passionate about the arts and visited and supported the museum frequently. The Michener Museum's board of trustees places the entire bequest into the endowment fund to help ensure the long-term financial stability of the museum.

In the spring the museum is the recipient of a $3 million grant from the Pennsylvania Governor's Redevelopment Assistance Capital Program. The grant is the largest the museum has ever received from Pennsylvania and is heralded by Governor Ed Rendell. The Michener Museum's increasing attendance, collections growth, and demand for educational activities are driving the need for facility improvements and expansion in Doylestown.

2007 Molli Conti is named president of the board of trustees.

The museum hires the architectural firm of RMJM Hillier to design a major expansion project in Doylestown.

2008 The James A. Michener Art Museum celebrates its twentieth anniversary and begins a program of free admission for all children on class trips as part of the celebration. Student attendance jumps to over eleven thousand annually in response.

Construction begins on a $12 million expansion project to add a major new gallery, additional art storage facilities, an educational center, and a new event center and to replace the HVAC, humidification, and air-filtration systems throughout the museum.

2009 Kevin S. Putman is named president of the board of trustees.

APPENDIX 2

1988 Inaugural Exhibition: *Twentieth-Century American Art*

Pennsylvania School of Landscape Painting of Bucks County

Paintings from the Mari and James A. Michener Collection of American Art

Contemporary Sculpture of the Region

1989 *Annual Bucks County Sculpture Exhibition*

Photographs by Aaron Siskind

Doylestown Art League's 1989 Juried Show

Full Circle: George Nakashima Retrospective

Antique Toys and Trains

Original Collages by James A. Michener

Vincent Ceglia: Paintings, Drawings, Assemblages

1990 *Ships and the Sea: Marine Paintings from the Cigna Museum and Art Collection*

Landscape Painting by Neil Welliver

The Art of Photography

Revolving Techniques: Thrown, Blown, Spun, and Turned

Annual Bucks County Sculpture Exhibition

Pennsylvania Impressionists of the New Hope School

Art under Our Feet

American Indian Portraits by Edward Curtis

A Forgotten Woman: Fern I. Coppedge Retrospective

Diverse Expressions of Blake Edwards

The Fellowship of the Pennsylvania Academy of the Fine Arts 93rd Annual Juried Exhibition of Academy Alumni

Weegee the Famous

1991 *New Hope Modernists, 1917–1950*

Paul Keene

In Our Circle

Annual Bucks County Sculpture Exhibition

An American Impressionist: Walter Elmer Schofield

Alan Magee: Retrospective

The Landscape Rediscovered: Selections from the Permanent Collection

A History of Art in Bucks County

Changing Visions of the American Landscape

A Picture of My World: Etchings by Jorg Schmeisser

1992 *Revolving Techniques: Clay, Glass, Metal, Wood*

The Landscape Rediscovered: Selections from the Permanent Collection

Rescuers of the Holocaust

Bucks County Artists Biennial I

Selections from the Permanent Collection

Michael A. Smith: A Visual Journey

1993 Permanent Exhibition: *James A. Michener: A Living Legacy*

Permanent Exhibition: *George Nakashima Memorial Reading Room*

Permanent Exhibition: *Visual Heritage of Bucks County*

The Great American Quilt Festival #3: Discover America / Friends Sharing America

Twentieth-Century American Art from the Mari and James A. Michener Collection

Mother and Child: The Last Portfolio of Henry Moore

Charles Hargens: Artist of the Old West

Woman's Work: Sculpture by Rhonda Roland Shearer

Catherine Jansen: Images from the Mind's Garden

Common Threads to Understanding: An Exhibit of the Names Project AIDS Memorial Quilt

Richard Upton: Ten Years of Italian Landscapes

1994 *Abstract Expressionism: Selections from the Michener Collection*

Clarence Holbrook Carter: Landscapes and Architectural Paintings

Dr. Kenneth Leiby: A Country Doctor and His Collection

Masterworks of American Impressionism: Edward Redfield and the New Hope Group

Life in the Valley: Photographs by Harold "Hal" Clark, Sara Maynard Clark, and Maynard Clark

Design '94 from the American Pewter Guild

Touch the Future: High School Artists from Bucks and Montgomery Counties

Wallace Herndon Smith Rediscovered

Annual Bucks County Sculpture Exhibition

John Weiss: The Face of Baseball

Werner Drewes: American Indians

Bucks County Artists Biennial II

Outdoor Sculpture Program: *Joe Mooney*

RAMs, ROMs, and Rainbows

The Artist Revealed: Photographs from the Collection of Peter Paone and Alma Alabilikian

A Collector's Eye: Depression-Era Paintings from the Collection of John Horton

Patterns of Vision: Tradition and Innovation in Contemporary Quilt Making

Inside Our Vault 1: R. John Foster

Inside Our Vault 2: The Eight

Inside Our Vault 3: Cooperative Painting Project

1995 *George Radeschi: Classic Vessels in Wood*

Kenjiro Nomura: An Artist's View of the Japanese-American Internment

Barry Snyder: Discover, Construct, Transform

John Fulton Folinsbee: A Retrospective

Contemporary Muse I: Dreams and Shadows: Wanda Chudzinski, Tom Ferris, David Hales, Carol May

Contemporary Muse II: It's a Small World: Sheila Letven, Joseph P. Peters, Deborah Wentworth

Outdoor Sculpture Program: *Christopher Cairns*

Katharine Steele Renninger: A Retrospective

Gary Erbe: Trompe L'Oeil Paintings

The Garber Mural and Selections from Regional Artists

Beveridge Moore: A Retrospective

Transformations: Four Contemporary Bucks County Artists: Jack Thompson, Susan Zoon, Judith Taylor, Tony Rosati

An Ocean Apart: Contemporary Vietnamese and American-Vietnamese Artists

The Dinosaur Portfolio: Paintings and Drawings by Philip Carlo Paratore

1996 *Images of Power: Balinese Painting*

American Naïve Paintings from the National Gallery of Art

William A. Smith: A Retrospective

Outdoor Sculpture Program: *Hans Van de Bovenkamp*

Abstract Expressionist Paintings from the Collection of Mari S. and James A. Michener

Three American Regionalists: Thomas Hart Benton, John Steuart Curry, and Grant Wood

Clarence Holbrook Carter and the American Scene

Milton Avery: Works on Paper

Newman's Gift: Fifty Years of Photography

Outdoor Sculpture Program: *Benbow Bullock*

The Tactile Vessel

Special Installation: *Richard Wedderspoon*

1997 Special Installation: *William Glackens*

Bucks County Invitational I: Selma Bortner, George Brooks-Hutton, Connie Coleman and Alan Powell, Robert Dodge, David Graham, Charney Harris

Contemporary Muse III: Surface, Symbol, Psyche: Contemporary Abstract Painting: Deborah Harris, Pamela Hoffman Taggart, Hisako Kobayashi, Bill Scott

Special Installation: *Mary Smyth Perkins Taylor*

Outdoor Sculpture Program: *Meryl Taradash*

Fred Staloff: Forty Years in Retrospect

Annual Bucks County Sculpture Exhibition

Special Installation: *Charles Sheeler*

Outdoor Sculpture Program: *Robert Ressler: Selections from Aluna*

Amish Quilts from the Museum of American Folk Art

Three Centuries of Japanese Printmaking

Michener Photographs and Artifacts

Special Installation: *Joseph Meierhans*

New Realities: Hand-Colored Photography, 1839 to the Present

Outdoor Sculpture Program: *Milan J. Kralik Jr.: The Color of Sky*

Masterpieces of Photography from the Merrill Lynch Collection

1998 *Healing Images, Healing Arts: Seventy-five Years of Care at the Doylestown Hospital*

Special Installation: *The Painter and His Apprentice: Portraits and History Paintings by Thomas and Edward Hicks*

Contemporary Prints from Rutgers Center for Innovative Print and Paper

Special Installation: *The Drawings of Alfred Bendiner*

Outdoor Sculpture Program: *Thom Cooney Crawford: Winged*

Bucks County Invitational II: Contemporary Woodworkers: Jeffrey Greene, Phillip Lloyd Powell, Mark Sfirri, Robert Charles Whitley II, Mira Nakashima-Yarnall

The Passionate Eye: Paintings by European and American Masters from Bucks County Collections

Machinery Can't Make Art: The Pottery and Tiles of Henry Chapman Mercer

A Legacy Preserved: The First Decade of Collecting at the Michener Museum

Outdoor Sculpture Program: *Molly Mason: Sun and Shadow: Sculpture in Stainless Steel, Bronze, and Aluminum*

Special Installation: *Joseph Pickett*

1999 *From Artist to Child: The Bucks County Intermediate Unit Collection*

Bucks County Invitational III: Contemporary Painters: Robert Beck, Alan Goldstein, Pat Martin, Eric Sparre

The Drawings of Harry Leith-Ross

Outdoor Sculpture Program: *Nils Kruger: Vitruvian Series*

The Philadelphia Ten: A Women's Artist Group, 1917–1945

From Soup Cans to Nuts: The Prints of Andy Warhol

Special Installation with the Mercer Museum: *An Edward Hicks Sampler*

Special Installation: *Picturing Washington: Icons and Images of America's Founding Father*

Outdoor Sculpture Program: *Barry Johnston*

Intimate Vistas: The Poetic Landscapes of William Langson Lathrop

Michener Millennium Design Award Installation: A Year and a Day by Charles Browning

Let Children Be Children: Lewis Wickes Hine's Crusade against Child Labor

Recent Gifts: Nineteenth- and Twentieth-Century Photographs from Alexander Novak and Family

2000 *The Jazz Age in Paris, 1914–1940*

No Ordinary Land: Encounters in a Changing Environment

Outdoor Sculpture Program: *Glenn Zweygardt: Roots, Haiku, and Beyond*

Bucks County Invitational IV: The Art Gene: George and Daniel Anthonisen, Robert and Jason Dodge, Emmet and Elijah Gowin, Barbara and Mark Osterman

Sublime Servers: A Celebration of Theatrical Possibilities at the Table

Grand Opening of the Children's Gallery: *A Celebration of the Art of Bucks County's Children*

John Goodyear: Works, 1950–2000

Special Installation: *The Drawings of Louis Bosa (1905–1981)*

Outdoor Sculpture Program: *Elizabeth Miller McCue: Haystacks in the Field*

The Secret World of Celia Reisman

In Line With Al Hirschfeld: An Al Hirschfeld Retrospective

Permanent Installation: *The Lenfest Exhibition of Pennsylvania Impressionism*

Children's Gallery: *Images of Self: Reflections in Visual and Language Art*

Outdoor Sculpture Program: *Jeanne Jaffe*

Carved, Incised, Gilded, and Burnished: The Bucks County Framemaking Tradition

Renny Reynolds: A Redfield Winter

2001 *The Photography of Alfred Stieglitz: Georgia O'Keeffe's Enduring Gift*

Children's Gallery: *A Child's View of Nature*

The Gift of Sympathy: The Art of Maximilian Vanka

Special Installation: *Solowey Unseen: Works by Ben Solowey from the Collection*

Outdoor Sculpture Program: *Ronn T. Mattia*

George Nakashima and the Modernist Moment

The Spirit of Abstraction: Contemporary Paintings from the Collection

Special Installation: *The Drawings of Robert Tieman*

Outdoor Sculpture Program: *Fred Schmidt*

Artists of the Commonwealth: Realism in Pennsylvania Painting, 1950–2000

Taking Liberties: Photographs by David Graham

2002 *Stylish Hats: 200 Years of Sartorial Sculpture*

Roy C. Nuse: Figures and Landscapes

Special Installation: *Painters from the New Hope Circle: Recent Acquisitions from the Lenfest Collection*

Outdoor Sculpture Program: *Maria A. Hall*

Bucks County Invitational V: Vincent Ceglia, Karl Karhumaa, Lisa Manheim, Claus Mroczynski

A Celebration of Voices: The Twenty-fifth Anniversary of A Woman's Place

Children's Gallery: *Come See Our World: Self, Family, and Community*

Special Installation: *Photographs by Michael A. Smith*

Walker Evans and James Agee: Let Us Now Praise Famous Men

Outdoor Sculpture Program: *Harry H. Gordon Stone Sculpture*

Earth, River, and Light: Masterworks of Pennsylvania Impressionism

Special Installation: *Retreating to Ideal Environments: Works of the New Hope Art Colony from the Estates of Henry A. Morof and Kenneth W. Gemmill*

The Berenstain Bears Celebrate: The Art of Stan and Jan Berenstain

Outdoor Sculpture Program: *Kate Brockman*

2003 *Randall Exon: A Quiet Light*

Children's Gallery: *Children Salute Levittown: A Celebration*

Levittown: A Home of Our Own

Special Installation: *Jack Rosen: Artist Portraits*

Six Continents of Quilts: The American Crafts Museum Collection

Outdoor Sculpture Program: *James Lloyd: Reflections of Embedded Images*

Japanese Prints from the Michener Collection

Special Installation: *The Michener Collects Alan Goldstein*

Children's Gallery: *Kids' Art: A Visual Language*

Latin Jazz: La Combinacion Perfecta

Outdoor Sculpture Program: *Ava Blitz: Zoo*

Camera Work: A Centennial Celebration

Alan Magee: Three Decades of Paintings, Sculpture, and Graphics

In the Shadows of Conflict: Works by Israeli and Arab-Israeli Youth

Outdoor Sculpture Program: *Won Jung Choi*

Grand Opening of Michener Art Museum New Hope

Michener Art Museum New Hope: *Coming Home: A Survey of New Hope Artists*

2004 *Emmet Gowin: Changing the Earth*

Rock On! The Art of the Music Poster from the '60s and '70s

Children's Gallery: *Retro Rhythms: A High School Perspective*

David Graham's Mule on the Street: Colorful Characters in Unexpected Places

Outdoor Sculpture Program: *Lorann Jacobs*

Mexican Folk Retablos: Images of Devotion

Michener Art Museum New Hope: *Edward W. Redfield: Just Values and Fine Seeing*

The Cities, The Towns, The Crowds: The Paintings of Robert Spencer

Children's Gallery: *A Visual Delight II*

Sandy Sorlien: House Photos

Outdoor Sculpture Program: *David Hayes*

Red, Hot, and Blue: A Salute to American Musicals

Red Grooms: Selections from the Complete Graphic Works, 1956–2000

Peter Paone: Imaginary Watercolors

Selma Bortner: Body of Work

Outdoor Sculpture Program: *Arleen Race Wolf*

Children's Gallery: *The Gift of Giving III*

Ken Wong: "Face to Face"

2005 *Michael Kenna: Impossible to Forget: The Nazi Camps Fifty Years After*

Michener Art Museum New Hope: *The Contemporary Eye: Judith Heep, Robert Ranieri, Mavis Smith, Marilyn Gordley, Susan Twardus, Valery Belenikin, Ann Lovett, Charlotte Schatz, Al Lachman, Ricardo Barros, Valerie Von Betzen, and David Ellsworth*

The Visual Literature of Bernarda Bryson-Shahn: Developing a Social Conscience

Playing Around: Toys Designed by Artists

Children's Gallery: *Child's Play*

Outdoor Sculpture Program: *Jonathan Hertzel*

That's All Folks! The Art of Warner Brothers Cartoons

Out in Front: Smarty Jones and Horse Raising in Pennsylvania

Michener Art Museum New Hope: *Selling Dreams: Film Posters, 1945–2005*

Emily Brown: The Evolving Landscape

Art in 2 Worlds: The Native American Fine Art Invitational, 1983–1997

Outdoor Sculpture Program: *Matthew and Jonathan Stemler*

Kathran Siegel: Still Life, Real Life

Michener Art Museum New Hope: *Objects of Desire: Treasures from Private Collections*

Paul Keene: His Art and His Legacy

Romare Bearden: Enchanter in Time

Outdoor Sculpture Program: *Kevin Forest*

New Orleans: A Beloved City: Photographs by Michael A. Smith

Louis Bosa: A Keen Eye and a Kind Heart

Children's Gallery: *The Gift of Giving*

2006 *Radical Vision: The Revolution in American Photography, 1945–1975*

Michener Art Museum New Hope: *Fashioning Art: Handbags by Judith Leiber*

Children's Gallery: *Our World: An Artist's Eye on Nature*

Ansel Adams: Celebration of Genius

An Enduring Gift: The Marguerite and Gerry Lenfest Collection

The Heart of Haiti: Andrea Baldeck

Outdoor Sculpture Program: *Mark Pettegrow: Equipose*

Bucks County Collects Bucks County: Twentieth Byers Bucks Fever Annual Art Exhibition

Michener Art Museum New Hope: *Poetry in Design: The Art of Harry Leith-Ross*

Show Business: Irving Berlin's Hollywood

Children's Gallery: *June Balloon*

Diane Burko: Flow

Todd Stone: Witness

Outdoor Sculpture Program: *Joe Mooney*

Duane Hanson: Real Life

Michener Art Museum New Hope: *Form Radiating Life: The Paintings of Charles Rosen*

Poetry in Design: The Art of Harry Leith-Ross

Children's Gallery: *The Gift of Giving*

Constructions: Photographs by Michael Becotte

Outdoor Sculpture Program: *Christoph Spath*

Wolfgang Roth: The Art of Theatre

2007 *Daniel Garber: Romantic Realist*

Children's Gallery: *Winter Exhibition*

Michener Art Museum New Hope: *Wild by Design: 200 Years of Innovation and Artistry in American Quilts*

James A. Michener: Traveller / Citizen / Writer

Aging in America: The Years Ahead

Outdoor Sculpture Program: *James Wolfe*

A Place in Time: The Shakers at Sabbathday Lake, Maine

Artists of the Commonwealth: Realism and Its Response in Pennsylvania Painting, 1900–1950

Children's Gallery: *June Balloon*

Michener Art Museum New Hope: *Gershwin to Gillespie: Portraits in American Music*

Fire and Ice: Marine Corps Combat Art from Afghanistan and Iraq

Soldier: Photographs by Suzanne Opton

Outdoor Sculpture Program: *Roger Loos*

Peter Rose: Excursions

Philip Pearlstein: The Dispassionate Body

Michener Art Museum New Hope: *Norman Rockwell in the 1940s: A View of the American Homefront* and *Charles Hargens: American Illustrator*

Children's Gallery: *The Gift of Giving*

2-4-6-8: American Cheerleaders and Football Players

Outdoor Sculpture Program: *John Costanza*

The Holy Experiment: Violet Oakley Mural Studies

2008 *Elsie Driggs: The Quick and the Classical*

Children's Gallery: *Winter Exhibition*

Michener Art Museum New Hope: *Robert Whitley: Beauty, Function, and Grace*

Outdoor Sculpture Program: *Susan Opie*

Color: Ten African American Artists

Lilli Gettinger: Memory Transformed

Elliot Erwitt: Dog Dogs

Michener Art Museum New Hope: *New Hope: Art and the River*

Intertwined: Contemporary Baskets from the Sara and David Lieberman Collection

Outdoor Sculpture Program: *James Fuhrman*

Cuba: Campo Adentro: Photographs by Susan Bank

Michener Art Museum New Hope: *Claus Mroczynski: Sacred Places of the Southwest*

Saving Face: Portraits from the Collection of Robert Infarinato

Children's Gallery: *The Gift of Giving*

Outdoor Sculpture Program: *Barry Parker*

Shifting Ground: Contemporary Landscapes by Paula Chamlee, Alan Goldstein, and Paul Matthews

Bernard "Ben" Badura (1896–1986)
Frame for George W. Sotter's
The Windybush Valley 1939
carved wood with gold-leaf gilding
42¼ x 54¼ x 2¼ inches
James A. Michener Art Museum. Gift
of Marguerite and Gerry Lenfest

Raymond Barger (1906–2001)
Transition 1965
bronze
21 x 25 x 6 feet
James A. Michener Art Museum. Gift
of the artist

Ricardo Barros (b. 1953)
Isaac Witkin 1996
carbon pigment digital print on paper
25⅜ x 24 inches
James A. Michener Art Museum.
Museum purchase funded by the Bette
and G. Nelson Pfundt Photography
Endowment

Walter Emerson Baum (1884–1956)
*South Side, Easton (Industrial Scene
Easton)* ca. 1940
oil on canvas
28 x 37 inches
James A. Michener Art Museum.
Gift of Marguerite and Gerry Lenfest

Michael Becotte (b. 1945)
Construction #339 2003
iris print on paper
28 x 36 inches
James A. Michener Art Museum.
Museum purchase funded by the Bette
and G. Nelson Pfundt Photography
Endowment

Selma Bortner (b. 1926)
Aida and the Mirror 1990
linoleum print on paper
30 x 36 inches
James A. Michener Art Museum.
Museum purchase funded by an
Anonymous Donor from the Bucks
Biennial I Exhibition

Louis Bosa (1905–1981)
Procession 1952
oil on canvas
40 x 62 inches
James A. Michener Art Museum. Gift
of Donald E. and Anna Bosa Mulligan

Rae Sloan Bredin (1880–1933)
After the Rain 1913
oil on canvas
30 x 40
James A. Michener Art Museum.
Museum purchase funded by the Janus
Society, the Beveridge Moore and Henry
Morof Trust, and John C. Seegers

Emily Brown (b. 1943)
Fond Farewell 2002
ink on paper
52 x 96 inches
James A. Michener Art Museum.
Museum purchase funded by
D. Kenneth Leiby

Howard Brunner (b. 1947)
Untitled (7924-21) 1979
gelatin silver print on paper
12¾ x 18¾
James A. Michener Art Museum.
Gift of the artist

Selma Burke (1900–1995)
Together 1975; cast 2001
bronze
74 x 49 x 9 inches
James A. Michener Art Museum.
Museum purchase with assistance
from John Horton, William Mandel,
the Bjorn T. Polfelt memorial fund,
Carolyn Calkins Smith, and the
Friends of Selma Burke

Diane Burko (b. 1945)
Vulcano from the Air 2001
oil on canvas
60 x 84 inches
James A. Michener Art Museum. Gift
of Jane Biberman

Lawrence Calcagno (1913–1993)
June 1961 1961
oil on canvas
59½ x 47½ inches
James A. Michener Art Museum. Gift of
Mari and James A. Michener

Clarence Holbrook Carter (1904–2000)
Over and Above Series (Fox) 1963
pencil, gouache, and feathers on paper
29½ x 21½ inches
James A. Michener Art Museum.
Michener Art Endowment Challenge
Gift of Mr. Wm. A. and Anne Stetson
Rawak

Charles Child (1902–1983)
*Study for the Bucks County Playhouse
Stage Curtain* ca. 1939
ink and watercolor on paper
24½ x 36½ inches
James A. Michener Art Museum.
Michener Art Endowment Challenge
Gift of Barbara S. and Sol Jacobson

Ed Colker (b. 1927)
*The Summons of Becoming: Poems by
René Char* 2007
translated by Mary Ann Caws with
hand-colored lithographs as pochoir
by Ed Colker
published by Haybarn Press, 2007
cloth portfolio book, printed letterpress
by Bradley Hutchinson; limited edition
9 x 14 inches
James A. Michener Art Museum.
Museum purchase

Morgan Colt (1876–1926)
Phillips Mill Barn n.d.
oil on canvas
19½ x 23½ inches
James A. Michener Art Museum. Gift of
Marguerite and Gerry Lenfest

Fern I. Coppedge (1883–1951)
Back Road to Pipersville n.d.
oil on canvas
38 x 40 inches

James A. Michener Art Museum. Gift of Robert J. Lillie

Fern I. Coppedge (1883–1951)
The Road to Lumberville (also known as *The Edge of the Village*)   1938
oil on canvas
18⅛ x 20⅛ inches
James A. Michener Art Museum. Gift of Ruth Purcell Conn and William R. Conn

Joseph Diano (1904–1987)
Wotan's Farewell   n.d.
stained glass
26¾ x 18 inches
James A. Michener Art Museum. Gift of Mrs. Helen Diano

Robert Dodge (b. 1939)
Four Plans   1994
acrylic, gold leaf on wood
19¼ x 37¼ inches
James A. Michener Art Museum. Museum purchase

Werner Drewes (1899–1985)
Sauk   1973
woodcut on Kochi paper
16¾ x 11⅛ inches
James A. Michener Art Museum. Michener Art Endowment Challenge Gift of Franz Geierhaas

Elsie Driggs (1898–1992)
Spotted Deer   n.d.
watercolor and pencil on paper
17 x 15 inches
James A. Michener Art Museum. Michener Art Endowment Challenge Gift of Margaret B. Oschman

Edmund Bruce Eckstein (b. 1943)
Basic Training, Fort Jackson South Carolina   1970, printed April 2007
gelatin silver print on paper
16 x 20 inches
James A. Michener Art Museum. Museum purchase funded by the Bette and G. Nelson Pfundt Photography Endowment

Edmund Bruce Eckstein (b. 1943)
May Day Rally (Philadelphia, May 1969)   1969, printed April 2007

gelatin silver print on paper
16 x 20 inches
James A. Michener Art Museum. Museum purchase funded by the Bette and G. Nelson Pfundt Photography Endowment

Rob Evans (b. 1959)
Cicada   1998–2000
acrylic and oil on board
40 x 120 inches
James A. Michener Art Museum. In trust to the James A. Michener Art Museum from Ms. Joyce Tseng

Randall Exon (b. 1956)
Beach House   2002
oil on canvas
36 x 36 inches
James A. Michener Art Museum. Museum purchase funded by the Janus Society

Susan Fenton (b. 1949)
Profile with Lizard   1992
handpainted, toned gelatin silver print on paper
24 x 24 inches
James A. Michener Art Museum. Museum purchase

John Fulton Folinsbee (1892–1972)
Bowman's Hill   1936–37
oil on canvas
34 x 50 inches
James A. Michener Art Museum. Gift of Marguerite and Gerry Lenfest

John Fulton Folinsbee (1892–1972)
River Ice   1935
oil on canvas
32¼ x 40 inches
James A. Michener Art Museum. Gift of the John Folinsbee Art Trust

Daniel Garber (1880–1958)
Garden Window   1946
etching and drypoint on paper
11⅜ x 10¼ inches
James A. Michener Art Museum. Gift of Mrs. John Garber

Daniel Garber (1880–1958)
Little Girl Knitting   1918
charcoal on laid paper

23¼ x 18¼ inches
James A. Michener Art Museum. Gift of Madelaine B. Garber

Daniel Garber (1880–1958)
Over at Byram   1940
oil on canvas mounted on Masonite
30 x 30 inches
James A. Michener Art Museum. Gift of Oliver Pearson

Daniel Garber (1880–1958)
Portrait of Frank Baisden   ca. 1923
charcoal on laid paper
23¼ x 17¾ inches
James A. Michener Art Museum. Gift of Madelaine B. Garber

Daniel Garber (1880–1958)
Springtime in the Village   1917
oil on canvas
30½ x 28½ inches
James A. Michener Art Museum. Gift of Marguerite and Gerry Lenfest

Daniel Garber (1880–1958)
A Wooded Watershed   1926
oil on canvas
129¼ x 257¼ inches
James A. Michener Art Museum. Acquired with a Legislative Initiative Grant awarded by Senator H. Craig Lewis

Lee Gatch (1902–1968)
Eastern Eagle   1958
oil on canvas
24½ x 33½ inches
James A. Michener Art Museum. Museum purchase funded by Anne and Joseph Gardocki

Alan Goldstein (b. 1938)
Upriver from Lumberville Walking Bridge II   ca. 1981
oil on canvas
65 x 96½ inches
James A. Michener Art Museum. Museum purchase funded by Anne and Joseph Gardocki

Harry Gordon (b. 1960)
Face   1982
white oak (stained)
72 x 48 x 48 inches
James A. Michener Art Museum. Gift of Philip and Muriel Berman

Emmet Gowin (b. 1941)
Nancy, Danville 1969
toned gelatin silver print on paper
5½ x 7 inches
James A. Michener Art Museum. Gift
of Emmet and Edith Gowin

David Graham (b. 1952)
P-Star Parking, Dallas, Texas 1997
dye coupler print on paper
19 x 19 inches
James A. Michener Art Museum.
Museum purchase

Jeffrey Greene (b. 1943)
Windsail Bench 2003
ash
52 x 86 x 46 inches
James A. Michener Art Museum.
Museum purchase funded by Shirley
Ellis, Carolyn Smith, and Sandra Hardy,
in Memory of Helen Bargeron Calkins

Robert Gwathmey (1903–1988)
End of Day 1943
oil on canvas
30 x 36 inches
James A. Michener Art Museum. Gift
of the John P. Horton Estate
Art © Estate of Robert Gwathmey /
Licensed by VAGA, New York, NY

Frederick William Harer (1879–1948)
Desk and Sidechair ca. 1930s
walnut with pear and ebony inlay and
upholstered slip seat
34½ x 38 x 22½ inches (desk),
30 x 17¾ x 17 inches (chair)
James A. Michener Art Museum.
Museum purchase funded by John C.
Seegers

Frederick William Harer (1879–1948)
Frame (known as "Spanish" frame) for
Edward W. Redfield's *Fleecydale Road*,
ca. 1930
carved wood with gold-leaf gilding and
paint
47⅛ x 58⅛ x 2½ inches
James A. Michener Art Museum. Gift
of the Laurent Redfield Family

H. Scott Heist (b. 1949)
Alexander Calder and White Cascades
1976
gelatin silver print on paper

20 x 16 inches
James A. Michener Art Museum.
Museum purchase

Thomas Hicks (1823–1890)
Portrait of Edward Hicks ca. 1850–52
oil on canvas
36⅛ x 29⅛ inches
James A. Michener Art Museum.
Museum purchase funded by Eleanor
K. Denoon, The Bella S. and Benjamin
H. Garb Foundation Inc., Mr. and Mrs.
Kenneth Gemmill, George S. Hobensack
Jr., Laurence D. Keller, William Mandel,
Members of Newtown Friends Meeting,
Olde Hope Antiques, Inc., Residents of
Pennswood Village, Eleanor and Malcolm
Polis, Ms. Leslie E. Skilton, Kingdon
Swayne, and Anonymous Donors

Eugene Higgins (1874–1958)
A Connecticut Ploughman n.d.
oil on canvas
26 x 33 inches
James A. Michener Art Museum. Gift
of the John P. Horton Estate

Catherine Jansen (b. 1950)
The Blue Room 1970
photosensitized cloth, photographic
dyes
James A. Michener Art Museum.
Museum purchase and partial gift from
artist

Paul Keene (b. 1920)
Variation on a Flute Player (Icon Series)
1985
acrylic on paper
41¼ x 29½ inches
James A. Michener Art Museum.
Museum purchase

Richard Kemble (1932–2007)
Another Beginning n.d.
color woodblock print on paper
18 x 23¾ inches
James A. Michener Art Museum. Gift
of George F. Korn

Richard Kemble (1932–2007)
Palenque 1974
color woodcut on paper
29½ x 21½ inches
James A. Michener Art Museum. Gift
of George F. Korn

Charles Klabunde (b. 1935)
Temptation of Saint Anthony 1964
etching on paper
36 x 58 inches
James A. Michener Art Museum.
Gift of Nancy M. Wolfe-Kennedy in
Memory of Martin F. Kennedy

Joan Klatchko (b. 1956)
Halloween 2000; printed 2002
chromogenic print on paper
14 x 20 inches
James A. Michener Art Museum. Gift
of the artist

Masami Kodama (b. 1933)
Six Triangles 1966
bronze
22½ x 53 x 21 inches; base 44 x 11 x
12 inches
James A. Michener Art Museum. Gift
of Edward Rosenthal

William Langson Lathrop (1859–
1938)
Chilmark Moor, Martha's Vineyard
1930
oil on canvas
25 x 30 inches
James A. Michener Art Museum. Gift
of Marguerite and Gerry Lenfest

William Langson Lathrop (1859–
1938)
Lathrop Sketchbook #9 1898–1904
pencil on paper
8½ x 5¼ inches
James A. Michener Art Museum. Gift
of Tom Buckley

William Langson Lathrop (1859–
1938)
Untitled (Landscape with Figure)
ca. 1897
oil on canvas
19 x 25 inches
James A. Michener Art Museum.
Michener Art Endowment Challenge
Gift of Malcolm and Eleanor Polis

Harry Leith-Ross (1886–1973)
Early Spring, New Hope Area n.d.
conté crayon on paper
3¼ x 5 inches
James A. Michener Art Museum. Gift
of Emily Leith-Ross

Harry Leith-Ross (1886–1973)
Factory Fire, Leiden, Holland 1965
conté crayon on paper
3 x 3¾ inches
James A. Michener Art Museum. Gift
of Emily Leith-Ross

Harry Leith-Ross (1886–1973)
Of Days Long Past ca. 1959
oil on canvas
20 x 40 inches
James A. Michener Art Museum.
Endowment Challenge Gift of Mrs.
Harry Leith-Ross

Barbara Lekberg (b. 1925)
Sea Wind II 1998
bronze
45 x 30 x 15 inches
James A. Michener Art Museum.
Museum purchase funded by a grant
from the Florsheim Art Fund

Joan Lindley (b. 1930)
Derby 1985–86
oil on canvas
48 x 66 inches
James A. Michener Art Museum.
Museum purchase

Arlene Love (b. 1936)
Maddy at 18 1976
polyester resin and fiberglass with
stainless steel support and wood base
46 x 19 x 23 inches
James A. Michener Art Museum. Gift
of William Hollis and Andrea Baldeck

James Lueders (1927–1994)
Untitled 1973
acrylic on canvas
76 x 96 inches
James A. Michener Art Museum. Gift
of Elizabeth Osborne

Alan Magee (b. 1947)
Countermeasure 2004
acrylic on canvas
50 x 75 inches
James A. Michener Art Museum.
Museum purchase funded by the Janus
Society
© Alan Magee, 2004

Alan Magee (b. 1947)
Wound 1995; printed 2004

giclée print on paper
22 x 17 inches
James A. Michener Art Museum.
Museum purchase

Reginald Marsh (1898–1954)
Italian Suite 1940
black ink, watercolor, and chinese
white on paper
27 x 39 inches
James A. Michener Art Museum. Gift
of the John P. Horton Estate
© 2009 Estate of Reginald Marsh / Art
Students League, New York / Artists
Rights Society (ARS), New York

Arthur Meltzer (1893–1989)
Summer Skies 1924
oil on canvas
22¼ x 32⅛ inches
James A. Michener Art Museum. Gift
of Remak Ramsay

Marlene Miller (b. 1935)
If I Can't Have You No One Will 2001
charcoal on paper
29¾ x 41¾ inches
James A. Michener Art Museum.
Museum purchase

R.A.D. Miller (1905–1966)
Lace Factory ca. 1935
oil on canvas
21 x 28 inches
James A. Michener Art Museum. Gift
of Marguerite and Gerry Lenfest

*George Nakashima Memorial Reading
Room* installed in 1993 in honor of
George Nakashima, furnishings by
Mira Nakashima-Yarnall (b. 1942):
Coffee Table, claro walnut burl, 1993
Conoid Lounge Chairs, claro and
English walnut, 1993
Open Back Bookshelf, cherry, 1993
Asa-no-ha Wall Cabinet, walnut, 1993
Hanging Wall Shelf, walnut, 1993
Shoji Screens, white cedar and
fiberglass, 1993

William A. Smith (1918–1989),
Portrait of George Nakashima
1988–89, oil on canvas, 43¾ x 41¼.
James A. Michener Art Museum.
Gift of Kevin Nakashima and Mira
Nakashima-Yarnall

Mary Brombacher Bowman
Bamboo Scroll 1998, watercolor on
rice paper, mounted on silk and cloth,
43 x 17 inches. James A. Michener
Art Museum. Gift of the artist

Lloyd Raymond Ney (1893–1965)
Study for New London Facets 1940
charcoal, graphite, and tempera on
gessoed laminated wood panel
69¼ x 167 inches
James A. Michener Art Museum.
Museum purchase and partial gift in
honor of Dr. Marvin and Muriel Sultz,
Elkins Park, PA

Kenneth Nunamaker (1890–1957)
Brook in Winter 1926
oil on canvas
44 x 50¼ inches
James A. Michener Art Museum. Gift
of Marguerite and Gerry Lenfest

Suzanne Opton (b. 1950)
Soldier: Benson—368 Days in Iraq 2005
gelatin silver print on paper
20 x 16 inches
James A. Michener Art Museum.
Museum purchase funded by the Bette
and G. Nelson Pfundt Photography
Endowment

Thomas P. Otter (1832–1890)
The Palisades at Nockamixon (also known
as *The Narrows of the Delaware*) 1875
oil on canvas
16¼ x 28¼ inches
James A. Michener Art Museum.
Gift of the Pennsylvania Academy of
the Fine Arts through the Bequest of
Kenneth W. Gemmill

Joseph T. Pearson Jr. (1876–1951)
The Twins: Virginia and Jane 1917
oil on canvas
60 x 72 inches
James A. Michener Art Museum. Gift
of Oliver Pearson

Guy Pène du Bois (1884–1958)
In the Courtroom n.d.
oil on canvas
17 x 24 inches
James A. Michener Art Museum. Gift
of the John P. Horton Estate

Stephen Perloff (b. 1948)
The Benjamin Franklin Bridge
1980/1981
gelatin silver print on paper
10½ x 13½
James A. Michener Art Museum. Gift
of Alexander Novak and Family

Phillip Lloyd Powell (1919–2008)
Fireplace ca.1956–58
walnut
97½ x 67 x 6 inches
James A. Michener Art Museum.
Museum purchase funded by the Janus
Society, Beveridge Moore and Henry
Morof Trust, and George C. Benson in
honor of his friend John Horton

Edward W. Redfield (1869–1965)
The Burning of Center Bridge 1923
oil on canvas
50¼ x 56¼ inches
James A. Michener Art Museum.
Acquired with funds secured by State
Senator Joe Conti, and gifts from
Joseph and Anne Gardocki, and the
Laurent Redfield Family

Edward W. Redfield (1869–1965)
Early Spring 1920
oil on canvas
38 x 50 inches
James A. Michener Art Museum. Gift
of Marguerite and Gerry Lenfest with
Assistance from Wachovia

Edward W. Redfield (1869–1965)
Fleecydale Road ca. 1930
oil on canvas
37½ x 49½ inches
James A. Michener Art Museum. Gift
of the Laurent Redfield Family

Edward W. Redfield (1869–1965)
The Trout Brook ca. 1916
oil on canvas
50 x 56 inches
James A. Michener Art Museum. Gift
of Marguerite and Gerry Lenfest

Celia Reisman (b. 1950)
Angel Awning 2000
oil on canvas
40 x 50 inches
James A. Michener Art Museum.
Museum purchase

Katharine Steele Renninger
(1925–2004)
*Morrell's Spinning Wheel and Wool
Winder* 1988
casein on linen canvas mounted on
Masonite
17⅝ x 23⅝ inches
James A. Michener Art Museum. Gift
of Mr. and Mrs. Joseph L. Wesley Sr.,
on the occasion of a tribute to George
Ermentrout

Tony Rosati (b. 1947)
Red Run 1995
monotype and watercolor on paper
5⅞ x 8 inches
James A. Michener Art Museum. Gift
of the artist

Charles Rosen (1878–1950)
Opalescent Morning ca. 1909
oil on canvas
32 x 40 inches
James A. Michener Art Museum. Gift
of Marguerite and Gerry Lenfest

Charles Rosen (1878–1950)
Quarry and Crusher ca. early 1930s
oil on canvas
32 x 40 inches
James A. Michener Art Museum.
Museum purchase funded by George
C. Benson in honor of his friend, John
Horton

Charles Rosen (1878–1950)
*The Roundhouse, Kingston,
New York* 1927
oil on canvas
30⅛ x 40¼ inches
James A. Michener Art Museum. Gift
of the John P. Horton Estate

Jack Rosen (1923–2006)
George Nakashima 1973
selenium toned print on paper
7 x 9 inches
James A. Michener Art Museum.
Museum purchase funded by Anne and
Joseph Gardocki

Charles Rudy (1904–1986)
Shorn Medusa 1959
bronze
26 x 22 x 15 inches

James A. Michener Art Museum. Gift
of Mrs. Charles Rudy

William Schwartz (1896–1977)
*Come to Me All Ye That Are Heavy
Laden* 1934
oil on canvas
40 x 50
James A. Michener Art Museum. Gift
of the John P. Horton Estate

Ben Shahn (1898–1969)
Study for Riker's Island Mural ca. 1934
tempera on paper
11 x 33 inches
James A. Michener Art Museum. Gift
of George Benson in Honor of John
Horton
Art © Estate of Ben Shahn / Licensed
by VAGA, New York, NY

Nelson Shanks (b. 1937)
Pigtails 2004
oil on canvas
19½ x 27¾
James A. Michener Art Museum.
Museum purchase funded by the Janus
Society
© 2004 Nelson Shanks

Mavis Smith (b. 1956)
Sink or Swim 2004
egg tempera on gesso panel
26 x 28 inches
James A. Michener Art Museum.
Museum purchase funded by Lorraine
Nevens Greenberg

Michael A. Smith (b. 1942)
Near Frenchtown, New Jersey 1973
gelatin silver chloride print on paper
7⅝ x 9⅝ inches
James A. Michener Art Museum.
Museum purchase funded by Anne
and Joseph Gardocki

William A. Smith (1918–1989)
Portrait of George Nakashima 1988–89
oil on canvas
43¾ x 41¼ inches
James A. Michener Art Museum.
Gift of Kevin Nakashima and Mira
Nakashima-Yarnall

Henry B. Snell (1858–1943)
The Barber's Shop   n.d.
oil on canvas
25 x 30 inches
James A. Michener Art Museum.
Michener Art Endowment Challenge
Gift of D. Kenneth Leiby

Ben Solowey (1900–1978)
Rae Seated (Green Dress)   1935
oil on canvas
45 x 36 inches
James A. Michener Art Museum.
Museum purchase funded by Anne and
Joseph Gardocki

George W. Sotter (1879–1953)
Brace's Cove   n.d.
oil on canvas
36 x 40 inches
James A. Michener Art Museum. Gift
of Marguerite and Gerry Lenfest

George W. Sotter (1879–1953)
Untitled (Night Snow Scene)   1949
oil on canvas
26 x 32 inches
James A. Michener Art Museum. Gift
of Marguerite and Gerry Lenfest with
Assistance from Wachovia

George W. Sotter (1879–1953)
The Windybush Valley   1939
oil on board
36 x 48 inches
James A. Michener Art Museum. Gift
of Marguerite and Gerry Lenfest

Robert Spencer (1879–1931)
A Gray Day   1912
oil on canvas
20 x 24 inches
James A. Michener Art Museum. Gift
of Marguerite and Gerry Lenfest

Henry Ossawa Tanner (1859–1937)
Christ Walking on the Water   ca. 1913;
print ca. 1950
etching on paper
7¼ x 9½ inches
James A. Michener Art Museum. Gift
of Samuel L. and Sheila Rosenfeld in
honor of John P. Horton

Jane Teller (1911–1990)
Celebration Totem   1978
maple, beech, oak, hemlock wood
91 x 40 x 38½ inches
James A. Michener Art Museum. Gift
of Ms. Eleanor Denoon

Jonathan K. Trego (1817–1901)
Anna Phillips Trego   ca. 1840
oil on fabric
25⅛ x 21⅜ inches
James A. Michener Art Museum.
Museum purchase funded by Margaret
M. Ahlum, Mrs. Lewis Hall, and
Henry Morof

Jonathan K. Trego (1817–1901)
Smith Trego   ca. 1840
oil on fabric
25⅛ x 21¼ inches
James A. Michener Art Museum.
Museum purchase funded by Margaret
M. Ahlum, Mrs. Lewis Hall, and
Henry Morof

William B. T. Trego (1859–1909)
Civil War Battle Scene   1887
oil on canvas
19¼ x 29½ inches
James A. Michener Art Museum.
Museum purchase funded by Anne and
Joseph Gardocki

Unknown
View of Almshouse   ca. 1900
oil on canvas
24 x 30⅛ inches
James A. Michener Art Museum.
Anonymous Gift

Gerd Utescher (1912–1983)
Elevators   1971
bronze
27 x 5¾ x 2 inches
James A. Michener Art Museum. Gift
of Anne D. Utescher

Maximilian Vanka (1889–1963)
Untitled (Miners, Pittsburgh)   1935
ink on paper
25½ x 20 inches
James A. Michener Art Museum. Gift
of Margaret Vanka Brasko

Charles Ward (1900–1962)
Goldie Peacock's House   1935
oil on canvas
28 x 32 inches
James A. Michener Art Museum.
Museum purchase and partial gift from
Kristina Ward Turechek and Mary
Ellen Ward

Charles Wells (b. 1935)
Whitman   1975
etching on paper
25 x 19½ inches
James A. Michener Art Museum.
Michener Art Endowment Challenge
Gift of Franz G. Geierhaas

Robert Whitley (b. 1924)
Throne Desk and Armchair   1999
curly maple, American black walnut,
bird's-eye maple, and dogwood with
ebony pegs
33½ x 64 x 32 inches (desk),
34 x 34¼ x 27 inches (armchair)
James A. Michener Art Museum. Gift
of Steve and Suzanne Kalafer and
Flemington Car and Truck Country
Family of Dealerships

Stephen Guion Williams (b. 1942)
Sunrise, Chosen Land   1972
gelatin silver print on paper
20¾ x 13⅞ inches
James A. Michener Art Museum.
Museum purchase funded by the Bette
and G. Nelson Pfundt Photography
Endowment

Isaac Witkin (1936–2006)
Waif's Anchors   1986
patinated bronze
119 x 102 x 36 inches
James A. Michener Art Museum. Gift
in memory of Robert V. Nesi by his
family

Michener Art Museum Collections Committee, 1988–2008

APPENDIX 4

William S. Aichele (2000)

Dana G. Applestein (1994–1995; 1997–2008)

Sheila Bass (1996)

Edward G. Biester Jr. (1991–2006;
Chair 1994–2000)

Doris Brandes (1990–2001)

Anthony C. Canike (1998)

Molli C. Conti (1999–2006)

Louis E. Della Penna (2005–2006)

Eleanor K. Denoon (1992–1996)

Edward Dougherty (2002–2004)

Zita Fitzsimmons (1999–2004)

Frank N. Gallagher, Esq. (1990–2008)

Joseph Gardocki (1995)

Elizabeth H. Gemmill (2005–2008)

J. Lawrence Grim Jr., Esq. (2000–2004)

Helene J. Hankin (1990–1991; 1994)

Linda B. Hodgdon (2001–2002)

Jane Jozoff (2006–2008)

M. Carole Knight (1999–2003)

Denver Lindley (1988–1989)

William H. Mandel (1997–2008;
Chair 2001–2004, 2008; Co-chair 2006–2007)

Norma Marin (1991)

Donald Mattern (1990–1991)

Mira Nakashima-Yarnall (2002–2008;
Chair 2005; Co-chair 2006–2007)

Polly Nesi (1990–1993)

Bonnie O'Boyle (2005–2008)

G. Nelson Pfundt (1998)

Katharine Steele Renninger (1988–2003;
Chair 1990–1993)

William Rieser (1996–2000)

Herman Silverman (1988–1989)

Leslie Skilton (1992–2008)

Carolyn Calkins Smith (1995–1998)

Robert J. Welch (2006–2008)

Margaret M. Ahlum

Lois R. Anderson

Bent Andresen

Dana G. Applestein

Artsbridge

Miss Jane Ashley

Marian Barford

Raymond Granville Barger

Irma Barness

Bellwether Foundation

Alfred and Elizabeth Bendiner
Foundation

George C. Benson

Ruth Berliner

Mr. Barney Berlinger

Philip and Muriel Berman

Benjamin D. Bernstein

Philip A. and Dianna T. Betsch

Jane Biberman

Anna Billa

Jane Bishop

Doris and Frederic Blau

Mrs. Louis Bosa

Mary Isabel Bosserman

Mary Brombacher Bowman

William E. and
Christina H. Bradshaw

Luther W. Brady, M.D.

Bradley Bransford

Margaret Vanka Brasko

Colleen Browning

Neil Brugmans

Howard Brunner

Tom Buckley

Thomas and Karen Buckley

Richard H. and Janes Nuse Burd

Friends of Selma Burke

Mrs. Robert Burns

Steven Caccavo

T. Sidney Cadwallader II

Elmer and Millie Case

Leone C. Cassidy

Barbara Ceglia and Scott MacNeill

Vincent Ceglia

Eric Cohn

Anne Spadea Combs

Ruth Purcell Conn and
William R. Conn

Dr. William Robson Conn

State Senator Joseph Conti

Nancy Ferris Cook

Vera Cook

Stanley P. Cope, M.D.

Mr. and Mrs. William Costello

David Crane

Dr. and Mrs. Thomas Crawford

Joyce Creamer

Carol Cruickshanks

Estate of Paul Darrow

Louis and Carol Della Penna

Eleanor K. Denoon

Mrs. Helen Diano

Morris Docktor

Robert Dodge

Marguerite Doernbach

Benjamin Eisenstat

Jane Sperry Eisenstat

Neil Ellenoff

Shirley Ellis, Carolyn Smith, and
  Sandra Hardy

Mr. and Mrs. Oscar Epstein

Gary T. Erbe

Rosina Feldman

Susan Fenton

Edward Fernberger Jr.

First National Bank of Newtown

Mary Jane Fitzpatrick

Richard Florsheim Art Fund

John Folinsbee Art Trust

Ms. Pearl Fox

Elaine Galen

The Bella S. and Benjamin H. Garb
  Foundation Inc.

John Garber

Mrs. John Garber

Madelaine B. Garber

Joseph and Anne Gardocki

Ms. Merryman Gatch

Franz G. Geierhaas

Kenneth W. Gemmill and
  Helen M. Gemmill

Kenneth W. Gemmill Estate

Nancy and Ralph Gesell

Alan Goldstein

Alan Goldstein and Judith Taylor

Marilyn Gordley

Emmet and Edith Gowin

David Graham

Paul Grand

Lorraine Nevens Greenberg

Dorothy Grider

Anita Gronendahl

Agnes and Robert Hagan

Elizabeth Hawley Haig

Mrs. Lewis Hall

H. Theodore Hallman Jr.

C. William Hargens III

Charles W. Hargens Jr.

H. Scott Heist

James Christopher Heist

Bob and Marcia Hider

Mr. and Mrs. Peyton L. Hinkle

Al Hirschfeld Foundation

George S. Hobensack Jr.

Hayward J. and Deborah D. Holbert

Donald Holden

William Hollis and Andrea Baldeck

John Horton

Ed and Sunny Howard

Phyllis N. Hulburd

Alice Hutchenson and Julia Fitzpatrick

Ginny Hutton

Barbara L. Ingerman

Ingham Springs Antiques

Barbara S. and Sol Jacobson

The Jannke Family

Paul Joseph Jannke and
  Helen Ernst Jannke

Catherine Jansen

Janus Society

Mr. and Mrs. Parry Jones

Nancy Blake Justis

Steve and Suzanne Kalafer

Anne Kaplan

Bruce Katsiff

Richard and Sylvia Kaufman

Judith Teller Kaye

Peter Keating

Paul Keene

The Keene Family

Laurence D. Keller

Stanton C. Kelton Jr.

School of Art Gallery, Kent State
  University

Barbara Bradshaw Kittredge

Joan Klatchko

Knight Engineering, Inc. and
  Tinsman Brothers, Inc.

Paul O. Koether

Kondrosky Family

George F. Korn

Allen W. Kratz and Paul J. Somerville

Harriet Kravitz

Roberta and Donald Kyle

The Lathrop Family

D. Kenneth Leiby

Mrs. Emily Leith-Ross

Marguerite and H. F. "Gerry" Lenfest

Richard S. Lennox

Ellen Leopold

Bernice Silverstein Lewis

Pennsylvania Legislative Initiative
  Grant awarded by H. Craig Lewis,
  State Senator Sixth District, Bucks
  and Philadelphia Counties

William Liebig

Dr. and Mrs. Seymour Lifschutz

Robert J. Lillie

David B. Long

Helen and Robert Lovett

Mrs. Margaret Lutz

Mr. and Mrs. Fletcher MacNeill

James Magill

Lee and Barbara Maimon

Gene Mako

William H. Mandel

Estate of Molly Marsh

Eva Martino

Phyllis Maxwell

Mr. and Mrs. Davis Meltzer

Mari and James A. Michener

Linda Milanesi

Lorna G. Miller

Marvin L. and Victoria Lee Miller

Beveridge Moore and
  Henry Morof Trust

Irving Beveridge Moore

Henry Morof

Henry Morof Estate

Mr. Henry Morris

Dennis Mueller

Ingrid W. Mueller

Donald E. and Anna Bosa Mulligan

Daniel I. and Barbara A. Murphy

Kevin Nakashima and
    Mira Nakashima-Yarnall

Robert V. Nesi by his family

Members of Newtown Friends Meeting

Alexander Novak and Family

Sally M. Nunamaker

The Nuse Family

Elizabeth Osborne

Margaret B. Oschman

W. Taylor and Elizabeth K. Oughton

The Helen Waite Papashvily Trust

Philip Paratore

Oliver Pearson

Pennsylvania Academy of the Fine Arts

Pennsylvania Art Conservatory

Brian H. Peterson

Bette and G. Nelson Pfundt

Pfundt Foundation

Bjorn T. Polfelt memorial fund

Bjorn T. Polfelt with assistance from
    the Fred Schmidt Estate

Malcolm and Eleanor Polis

Julia B. Pool

Mrs. Michael Procyk

Remak Ramsay

Mr. William A. and
    Anne Stetson Rawak

Dorothy H. Redfield and
    Patricia Redfield Ross

Laurent Redfield Family

Eva Reichl

Wally Reinhardt

Katharine Steele and
    John S. Renninger

Dr. and Mrs. J. David Rockafellow

Tony Rosati

Mrs. Lillian Rose

Jack Rosen

Mr. and Mrs. Samuel L. Rosenfeld

Edward Rosenthal

Wolfgang Roth

Mrs. Charles Rudy

Donald and Joyce Rumsfeld

Frances Salberta

Estate of Jennie E. Savidge

Mrs. Morris Savidge

Roz and Henry Schaeffer

Charlotte Schatz

Jorg Schmeisser

Florence Platt Schoffhausen

John C. Seegers

Natalie Shapiro

Tanis Garber Shaw

Mrs. Olive P. Sheppard

Hannah H. R. and
    Samuel R. Shipley III

The Silverman Family

Ann and Herman Silverman

Mrs. Mattiemae Silverman

Herbert Simon

Mrs. Dorothy Simpson

Carolyn Calkins Smith

Michael A. Smith

Ann and Martin Snyder

Alan Sockloff

Stirling Spadea and
    Anne Spadea Combs

Louise Zimmerman Stahl

Jacob Stone

Janet L. and Lawrence C. Stone

Dr. Marvin and Muriel Sultz

Ellen Pearson Sutton

Walter Teller

Mrs. J. Arnold Todd

Trivellini Family

Mrs. Lynn D. Trusdell

Joyce Tseng

Kristina Ward Turechek and
    Mary Ellen Ward

Frank Ulrich

Union National Bank

Anne D. Utescher

Hendrik Van Oss

Mrs. Mary Carter VanZanten

Wachovia Bank

Herbert E. Ward Estate

Mr. Herbert Ward

Margaret Weil

June Miller Weingarten

Anita Weschler Estate

Mr. and Mrs. Joseph L. Wesley Sr.

Nancy M. Wolfe-Kennedy

Dorothy Stauffer Wood

Nancy Wasell Work

Katharine Worthington-Taylor

Greg Wyatt

APPENDIX 6
William H. Mandel

In the year 2000, to balance the Michener Art Museum's operating budget, it became necessary to cut out the modest funding for acquisitions that had been a normal part of the budget. I was on the collections committee and thought it would be a good time to raise income that would be used exclusively for acquiring art.

Pierre Rosenberg, the director of the French Louvre, happened to retire that same year, and in a *New York Times* interview he said, "A museum that does not acquire is a museum that dies."

With Rosenberg's words as inspiration, I consulted two friends: Harold Holzer, vice president/director of Public Information at the Metropolitan Museum of Art, and Martha Fleischman, owner and president of Kennedy Galleries in New York City. After those meetings I decided that I would organize a "club," called the Janus Society, the purpose of which would be to raise funds specifically for acquisitions. Annual contributions would be $5,000, and I was going to try to recruit a ten-person founding group. To begin the long pull, I sent a check for $5,000 to the museum on December 1, 2001.

There would be no membership campaigns for the Janus Society. It would grow through one-on-one contact with those friends of the museum who have an interest in the continuing excellence and expansion of our core collections. In April 2002 Carolyn Calkins Smith got the ball rolling by becoming a member, followed in June by Nelson Pfundt. That same year Cindy and Al Ruenes, M.D., joined the society.

The extraordinary Princeton photographer Emmet Gowin, who lives in Newtown and is a remarkable lecturer, offered to speak to the Janus Society about the art of photography. Jock Reynolds, director of the Yale University Art Gallery, arranged for me to buy Gowin's books from the Yale University Press to distribute to our members. The gathering was a great success and convinced David Lewis, M.D., one of the thirty guests at the luncheon, to become a Janusian.

Betsy Gemmill, a wonderful person who has devoted a great deal of her time and generosity to other good causes, became the fifth member of the society, and her support

helped us buy the first significant work of art for the collection using Janus funds exclusively: Randall Exon's *Beach House.* Similarly, Alan Magee, a world-renowned artist with strong Bucks County connections who had been featured in a major exhibit at the Michener, was commissioned by the museum to paint *Countermeasure,* a beautiful depiction of stones paid for by the Janus Society. Janus funds also were used to purchase Rae Sloan Bredin's *After the Rain,* which was quickly followed by Nelson Shanks's *Pigtails* and Mark Pettegrow's bronze sculpture *Mariposa.*

Lou Della Penna, a renowned collector of Pennsylvania impressionism, is a man who travels a great deal and always comes home with art. Lou joined the Janus Society along with his wife, Carol, as did Jane and Mal Jozoff, who live in Paradise Valley, Arizona, and at their beautiful house and property in Bucks County. Recent Janusians Christine and Noel Figueroa, who have all kinds of animals on their property, are also dedicated to the Michener's work with children and families.

The Michener is now in the process of expanding. Workers are busy digging and pouring foundations, putting up walls, and dividing spaces, all with the purpose of collecting, preserving, and exhibiting the art of the Bucks County region. The funds provided by the Janus Society will continue to advance this mission by acquiring work that will be on the museum's walls and in its vault for generations to come.

JANUS SOCIETY MEMBERS

Robert Barbanell
Louis E. and Carol Della Penna
Christine Soderman and Noel Figueroa
Elizabeth H. Gemmill
Jane and Mal Jozoff
David G. Lewis, M.D.
William H. Mandel
The Pfundt Foundation/G. Nelson Pfundt
Kevin S. Putman
Dr. and Mrs. Albert Ruenes
Carolyn Calkins Smith
The Warwick Foundation

MICHENER ART MUSEUM BOARD OF TRUSTEES, 1988–2009

APPENDIX 7

MEMBERS OF THE BOARD OF TRUSTEES, 2009

Herman Silverman, *Chairman Emeritus*
William S. Aichele, *Chairman*
Kevin S. Putman, *President*
Louis E. Della Penna, *Vice President*
Albert W. Pritchard Jr., *Treasurer*
Elizabeth Beans Gilbert, *Secretary*

F. David Aker, Ph.D.
Dana G. Applestein
William F. Brenner
Robert L. Byers
Anthony C. Canike
Edward Fernberger Jr.
Charles H. Gale Jr.
Frank N. Gallagher, Esq.
Elizabeth H. Gemmill
Jane Jozoff
M. Carole Knight
Bruce Norman Long
William H. Mandel
Sydney F. Martin
Bonnie O'Boyle
G. Nelson Pfundt
Tom Scannapieco
Frederick E. Schea
Virginia Sigety
Leslie Skilton
John H. Slaymaker
Robert J. Welch

MEMBERS OF THE BOARD OF TRUSTEES, 1988–2009

William S. Aichele (1995–present)
F. David Aker (2008–present)
Dana G. Applestein (1992–present)
Jennifer Barclay (1997–1999)
Marian Barford (1987–1989)
Sheila Bass (1988–1996)
Edward G. Biester Jr. (1990–2006)
Doris Brandes (1987–2003)
William F. Brenner (1987–present)
Robert L. Byers (1988–present)
Anthony C. Canike (1992–present)
Molli Conti (1998–2008)
Theodore Croll (1988)
Louis E. Della Penna (2004–present)
Eleanor K. Denoon (1992–1996)
Edward J. Dougherty (2002–2004)
Evelyn Doyle (1998)
Neil Ellenoff (1999–2004)
George Ermentrout (1988–1994)
Peter Farmer (1988–1989)
Edward Fernberger Jr. (2002–present)
Zita Fitzsimmons (1998–2000)
Charles H. Gale Jr. (1992–present)
Frank N. Gallagher (1988–present)
Joseph Gardocki (1995–1996)
Elizabeth H. Gemmill (2004–present)
Elizabeth Beans Gilbert (1993–present)
J. Lawrence Grim Jr. (1998–2004)
Helene Hankin (1987–2000)
Maureen Harvey (2005–2007)
Richard Hirschfield (2005–2008)
Linda Hodgdon (1996–2002)
Earl Jamison (1988–1989)

Jane Jozoff (2006–present)
M. Carole Knight (1996–present)
Denver Lindley (1987–1988)
Bruce Norman Long (2008–present)
Jack Lyons (1990–1992)
William H. Mandel (1997–present)
Bernie Mangiaracina (1987–1988)
Nora Marin (1990–1992)
Sydney F. Martin (2008–present)
Don Mattern (1987–1991)
Irving W. McConnell (2005–2007)
Jan Michael (2004–2007)
Mira Nakashima-Yarnall (2002–2007)
Polly Nesi (1989–1994)
Bonnie O'Boyle (2005–present)
G. Nelson Pfundt (1992–present)
Albert W. Pritchard Jr. (1990–present)
Kevin S. Putman (1992–present)
Steve Raab (1987–1988)
Katharine Steele Renninger (1987–2004)
Albert Renzi (1989–1992)
William Rieser (1987–2003)
Bryce Sanders (1999–2004)
Tom Scannapieco (2007–present)
Frederick E. Schea (2009)
Dianne Semingson (1988–1997)
Virginia Sigety (2005–present)
Herman Silverman (1987–present)
Leslie Skilton (1992–present)
John H. Slaymaker (2005–present)
Carolyn Calkins Smith (1989–2006)
Robert J. Welch (2006–present)

MICHENER ART MUSEUM STAFF, 2009

Diane Ambrose, *Manager of Development Events and Volunteers*

Ruth Anderson, *Assistant Curator of Education*

Basil Antrobus, *Security Officer*

Eleanor Bauer, *Membership Assistant*

Birgitta H. Bond, *Librarian and Database Coordinator*

Edward J. Borneo, *Facility Assistant*

Bryan Brems, *Preparator*

Hollie Brown, *Director of Visitor Services and Retail Operations*

Sara Hesdon Buehler, *Collections Registrar*

Frank Charlton, *Security Officer*

Candace Clarke, *Communications Manager*

Kevin Clarke, *Front Desk Staff*

Sarah Colins, *Development Associate*

Melissa Easton-Sandquist, *Education Coordinator*

Judy Eichel, *Executive Assistant to the Director*

Jack Emerson, *Security Officer*

Valerie Friedman, *Front Desk Staff*

Anita Greenspan, *Front Desk Staff*

Carole Q. Hurst, *Senior Development Officer*

Erika Jaeger-Smith, *Associate Curator of Exhibitions*

Michael Jayne, *Assistant Facility Manager*

Bruce Katsiff, *Director/CEO*

Constance Kimmerle, *Curator of Collections*

Kristy Krivitsky, *Associate Curator of Contemporary Art*

Dar Landes, *Director of Accounting*

Margaret MacDonald, *Development Associate, Corporate Business Partners Program*

Kathleen Malloy, *Coordinator for Art On The Move*

Faith McClellan, *Exhibitions Registrar*

Kathleen McSherry, *Director of Marketing*

Bettina A. Murdoch, *Development Officer*

Florrie Nebiolo, *Front Desk Staff*

Nina Paratore, *Front Desk Staff*

Brian H. Peterson, *Gerry and Marguerite Lenfest Chief Curator*

Susan Plumb, *Director of Educational Outreach and Diversity*

Chuck Quaste, *Director of Protection Services and Building Operations*

Adrienne N. Romano, *Curator of Education*

Pamela Sergey, *Manager of Visitor Services and Museum Shop*

Susan Sherman, *Children's Gallery Coordinator*

Zoriana Siokalo, *Director of Programs*

Maureen Skorupa, *Front Desk Staff*

Tana Steen, *Security Officer*

Deborah Velardi, *Bookkeeper*

Joan Welcker, *Membership and Information Technology Manager*

Sean Wells, *Exhibitions Registrar*

Susan White, *Front Desk Staff*

Jeffrey Whittock, *Security Officer*

Gilbert Winner, *Facility Manager*

Louise Zappulla, *Curatorial Assistant*